Compassion

Compassion

Yes, We Can Have It Again

TRAVIS A. MILLER

RESOURCE *Publications* • Eugene, Oregon

COMPASSION
Yes, We Can Have It Again

Copyright © 2022 Travis A. Miller. All rights reserved. Except for brief quotations in critical publications or reviews, no part of this book may be reproduced in any manner without prior written permission from the publisher. Write: Permissions, Wipf and Stock Publishers, 199 W. 8th Ave., Suite 3, Eugene, OR 97401.

Resource Publications
An Imprint of Wipf and Stock Publishers
199 W. 8th Ave., Suite 3
Eugene, OR 97401

www.wipfandstock.com

PAPERBACK ISBN: 978-1-6667-4875-8
HARDCOVER ISBN: 978-1-6667-4876-5
EBOOK ISBN: 978-1-6667-4877-2

07/25/22

Contents

Introduction | vii

1. What I Believe In (and Why I Believe It) | 1
2. The Smallest Acts Have the Largest Effects | 11
3. Humility and Death of the Self | 17
4. Being Selfish and Selfless with Grace | 25
5. The Duality of Being Grateful | 33
6. A Sam's Club-Sized God | 39
7. Truth AND Consequences | 47
8. "I Don't Know" is Okay | 57
9. At Your Service | 63
10. I Can Do This All Day | 69
11. All Things Being Equal | 76
12. This is Only a Test | 85
13. Love in the Time of Screaming Hot Takes | 93
14. Forgive Even When You Can't Forget | 99
15. The Difference Between Knowledge and Wisdom | 106
16. Peace & Community Can Accomplish Greatness | 114
17. . . . And Justice for All | 122
18. Speaking of All These Yesterdays | 128
19. Thank You for Listening | 134

About the Author | 139
Acknowledgements | 141

Introduction

MEL GIBSON'S "THE PASSION of the Christ" is a deeply polarizing film. It holds an approval rating of roughly 50% on Rotten Tomatoes, which seems to jibe with pretty much anything in American society at this moment. Some view it as a cinematic masterpiece that accurately portrays the suffering that Christ endured as He went to His death. Others are appalled by the graphic violence that, while fairly accurate to the extreme punishments in the first century Roman Empire, were a bit much for modern audiences to stomach even before you factor in the cries that it was an anti-Semitic film.

I only saw the film once, but the moment that stood out to me the most was buried deep in the film as a flashback. It involved a much younger Jesus, working as a carpenter with His mother long before His public ministry. In the scene, Jesus is making a table that is more in line with the way people sit in the modern day than they did in Judea at the time. He even had to demonstrate how one would sit at the table to Mary.

It is such a simple scene, but I feel it is important because it shows Christ's humanity. In it, He demonstrates His idea that differs from a common practice but explains it in a simple and caring way. It is a warm moment, a touching one, a *human* one from someone who is supposed to be equal to God. I think it illustrates His compassion so well.

When I started writing this book, I wasn't sure where it was going. I felt the idea of it as a subtle calling. I was preparing to go on a vacation that would have most of my core family on sharing a beach house for a week.

Compassion

My wife and son would be there along with my sister, her husband, and their adult sons (one with his girlfriend along), as well as my parents. It was a trip where we would be together in one place all together for more than a day, something that rarely happens anymore and given the age of my parents, could become even more rare in the future. It was to a quiet island community in southern Alabama and would provide a place to slow down and reflect.

Before going on this trip, I felt a nudge within me: I was to take a composition book and write on compassion. I didn't know which direction it would take. I didn't have a grand outline in mind. If anything, I kind of felt like I was supposed to sit down with my coffee on the first morning and be like, "Okay, Lord, I am here. Now what?"

Yes, that is exactly how it started. I finished breakfast, grabbed the notebook and a cup of coffee, and sat down overlooking the Gulf of Mexico from the balcony of the beach house. I even prayed, "Okay, I am here. What is the next step?" The old school act of putting physical pen to paper felt like a tremendous first step. To that point I had been subtly pushed to leap, but the contact of pen to paper was the actual leap.

The first line I wrote was "There is a lack of compassion in the world on all sides." In the United States, there really isn't even an "all" sides. There are two. As a society we have come to a point where every issue, every question, everything where you can have an opinion has to be on one side or the other. It may stem from the more interconnected world we live in, but you see it every day. As an avid sports fan I see it in such mundane things as "Paul George is a great basketball player and is only doing what is best for his career, "and "Paul George sucks and he abandoned the Indiana Pacers, so forget him."

We have also seen, quite starkly, how this carries over to larger issues with the recent COVID-19 pandemic. The entire time since the pandemic began in early 2020 it has been viewed through a lens of one side or the other. Only the United States could politicize a global health crisis instead of coming together for the greater good. We could agree on defeating the Nazis in World War II, but policies regarding public health changed if you crossed an imaginary line separating states, mostly because on one side of the line you had a different political party in charge as opposed to the other side of the line.

If one side believed in the science and facts presented the other side saw it as an attack on freedom. If one side said "maybe we should open

Introduction

things up early" the other would retreat and say they were mad and self-serving. Once vaccines were available even that became a political issue, as it was "patriotic" to resist getting vaccinated or you were "in a cult" if you chose not to get vaccinated, with one's political leanings factoring heavily into the decision either way.

Throughout all this, there has been a lack of compassion, and it goes beyond just scoring points for whatever political side you are on. It has exposed a deeply rooted failing that many Americans have in lacking both compassion and empathy.

I am just as guilty of this as anyone. For a very long time I held a view of, "You must be responsible for your own personal actions at all times." That was a very black and white worldview. I grew up in a very conservative part of the country and throughout my adolescence and early adulthood I would be described as extremely conservative. I was raised in the Evangelical (note the large "E") environment, but I began to change in my late 20s. I became much more middle of the road. I opened my eyes to larger issues, and in that, I feel I learned to be more compassionate. Encouraged to think critically and make up my own mind about things, that is what I did. I was never perfect in learning this even to this day, but I cannot help but see that this nation needs a return to feeling things like compassion and basic human empathy for other people while still having responsibility for individual actions. They do not have to be mutually exclusive.

I say this because the things that have stood out to me in my own reading of the Bible were the simple aspects of the life of Jesus: Compassion. Empathy. Humility. Servanthood. Grace. Even though these are things Christ Himself exemplified, they are forgotten or even viewed as weaknesses by many. One of the best books I have read recently was *Jesus & John Wayne: How White Evangelicals Corrupted a Faith and Fractured a Nation* by Kristen Kobes Du Mez. It was a fascinating book because, in many ways, I lived it. I grew up in the hyper-masculinized church where Jesus was a warrior and anyone who thought otherwise was a lost heathen in need of being saved by the Gospel. If we didn't evangelize people to our specific view of the Christian faith then we were losing people to hell, and anyone outside of our specific view was "of the world" and not to be trusted. The entire culture *Jesus and John Wayne* documents how the Christian Right rose to become a political force in America is one I am deeply familiar with. I was inside it growing up. [1]

Compassion

The book fascinated me because many of the morals and values that have shaped my current worldview came from this culture, yet I feel like it has become deeply lost by straying away from those basic principles of Jesus. It has felt like a betrayal, and I still struggle to maintain cordial relationships with these people. It is because of what I was taught that I now feel this way and why I feel a calling to write on compassion, as well as many other attributes of Jesus.

We are more than two sides. I believe that as a society we can be better. I still hold my Christian beliefs, but I do not see them as some exclusive club that once you are in, you are free to judge and exclude others if they do not believe in the exact same way. Matthew 20:28 says: "just as the Son of Man did not come to be served, but to serve, and to give his life as a ransom for many." There are many examples where Jesus could have taken dynamic actions, but instead he served. He was compassionate. He was humble. He listened.

We can get back to that. We can be better.

It is that desire to be better that motivates me to write this. I don't feel I have any great authority on theological matters. I am just a guy who grew up in the church and has taken many of its core tenets to heart, but has seen where the church itself, its followers, and the world writ large has lost sight of what Christ actually preached. I am not perfect in any way, shape, or form, nor do I feel like an authority on much of anything not sports related. Take this work as being "a guy with some thoughts and some receipts to back those thoughts up." If you're cool with that, welcome aboard.

To me: Christ had a very simple message: He was the sacrifice needed to make things right with God and mediator between God and our fallen world for all of us. All we have to do is accept that sacrifice. I pull this from 1 Timothy 2:5-6 where the Apostle Paul wrote: "For there is one God, and there is one mediator between God and men, the man Christ Jesus, who gave himself as a ransom for all, which is the testimony given at the proper time."

Think of the simplicity in that statement and how that is the supreme example of compassion. Christ is that one mediator. As we see elsewhere in Scripture, He is God become flesh. In each of the four Gospels we see a different view of Jesus, but they each touch on both his humanity and he divinity. I am not here to argue whether Jesus was fully God, fully man, half God, half man, 53.4% God/46.6% man, or anything like that. The main idea is that He is the mediator between God and man.

Introduction

Jesus does what we cannot do ourselves: He delivers the ultimate act of compassion by going before the throne itself in order to speak for us. He paid the price for us, and all we have to do is accept it. That's it. There isn't anything else in there about where you must live, who you need to vote for, what causes you support, or anything else. There are absolutely guides to "holy living" throughout the rest of the Bible. There are attitudes we are called to have and actions we are called to take as gratitude for His mediation for us, but the basic idea is simple: Christ died for us, accept it, and we're cool. It is unconditional. It is for all of us, all as a gift given freely from the God of the universe.

This idea was the impetus for this work, but it shows itself in so many ways. That is what I would like to focus on as I go further in this, and I hope that it opens your eyes to see that regardless of background or beliefs, we can have compassion again. We see it in the following ways:

- **Grace**—As we are promised, Christ's grace is infinite, and from my lived experience, I am thankful for that.
- **Gratefulness**—Yes, we should be grateful for His sacrifice, but I think Christ is grateful to have us along for the ride. I appreciate the invite!
- **Justice**—We have numerous examples from Christ's life where He is just and fair. Remember: He is the ultimate mediator.
- **Humility**—This has always been the most important aspect of Christ to me, and one that I think many people often forget.
- **Perseverance**—This is the heart of my favorite verse: James 1:4. Christ shows it by constantly seeking us. Out of gratitude we seek Him as a result.
- **Equality**—Christ died for all. Enough said.
- **Love**—It is the love of Christ for us that saves us.
- **Truth**—When you look at the Gospels Christ often spoke the truth, even when people did not want to hear it.
- **Service**—This links with the humility aspect. Christ's service for us stands out to me because He represents God's attempt to serve for us.
- **Forgiveness**—This is linked to grace, as he is perfect in forgiving us.
- **Patience**—Have you seen humanity? It has to take infinite patience to deal with us if you're God.

Compassion

This is going to be quite a journey. Some of it is going to be serious. Some of it is going to be irreverent and off the cuff. Some of it is going to be very raw from my own experiences and failures. Hopefully some of it is even a little funny because God has a sense of humor (at least I hope so. Otherwise, I am very screwed).

I remember once being told that prayer is not all about finding flowery words and the right way to say things. It is about having a conversation with God. I mean, it's God. He's the Creator of the entire Universe. That is awe-inspiring, but I have found my best time spent in prayer is just being unfiltered and saying what's on my mind as if I am talking to someone else. It is a cathartic experience.

That's what I want to try and do in this work. I want to be honest and up front. You've taken a chance on me by picking up this book, so I already thank you for it. I am glad that I have piqued your curiosity enough to jump in a little further. I am sure there are things you're not going to agree with me on, but I know if we were sitting there and having an open conversation there are things I wouldn't agree with you on. That's fine. I talk to Indiana University basketball fans all the time and aside from that they seem like reasonable people.

This book is probably going to make a lot of people uncomfortable. It is even making me uncomfortable because it represents a big leap of faith. It is an attempt to reconcile not only what I see as a wrong in the world, but a wrong within me. If I am to ask others to feel compassion, I have to first seek it myself. That's not easy. There is going to be a lot of raw pain put down, some coarse language, and some blunt opinions. There can also be some fun in it, because we connect through stories.

This is a chance to put some thoughts out in the world and see if they can bear some fruit in the form of getting us back where we need to go. We can be better as a society, and it is time to seek that out by being compassionate again.

So welcome aboard or strap in. I hope it is at least a little enlightening either way.

1

What I Believe In (and Why I Believe It)

IF THIS BOOK HAD an origin story it would begin with a holdup at gunpoint involving my father when I was an infant. I wasn't there, but my dad was a small business owner and was working late one night when he was held up while closing his business. As he tells the story, there was a great moment of fear for him because the barrel of the gun was so close to his face, he said he could see the shotgun slugs. He believes that if he had not become a Christian before that moment, he would have been shot and killed

I owe much of my faith to my father. I have a deep appreciation for it as well. While we were a Midwestern church-going family growing up it never felt forced. The way he imparted his faith on me was with a gentle guidance. He shared his faith unabashedly, but he never forced me. The way that I look at it is he planted the seeds of Christ's teachings, but as I grew, he trusted me to learn for myself and make up my own mind. While I was raised in the church, I still had freedom to pursue other interests.

The greatest lesson he tried to teach me was, "You need to know what you believe and why you believe in it, otherwise the world will tell you what to believe and why to believe in it." It has been one of the guiding principles of my life since probably around the time I was 11 years old. It is a phrase that has had a constant evolution, however. What it meant during one period of my life was different than what it means now. I suppose that in 20 or 30 years it will become something different still.

Compassion

When I was a teenager, it meant obedience. I believed in Christ because it was what I was supposed to do. It was the faith of my youth and if I didn't believe I was going to hell. Any doubt in this was seen as a weakness in faith and I needed to try that much harder. If this book is about compassion, I did not have it for myself because of this view. Everything was black and white. If it wasn't right, it was 100% wrong. If I did something wrong, there was to be no forgiveness because I was supposed to be smarter than that. Over time, this only led to loads of guilt that I carried around for years, often over the slightest things. I completely missed the point that *none* of us are good enough on our own merits, which is why we need the grace of God in the first place.

This attitude would linger into my 20s, but it began to thaw around the time I got married. My wife is from Miami, which is an entire world different from the Midwest. The first time I went down there to visit it was a shock to the system. It is a grand mixture of cultures, flavors, styles, and more. In many ways it is its own little world (think Florida Man, only Miami is the "Florida" of Florida), one that was a wakeup call to my Midwestern sensibilities.

Regarding my faith, I was still wedded to the "Christianity is the only way," but my experiences with it there were much different, as the culture shock was significant. One instance that stood out to me was simply walking around a shopping mall in what is the highest Spanish speaking city in the United States per capita. For the first time in my life I, a white male, was the minority. I was getting lots of looks. I eventually said something quietly about it to my future wife and she said, "that's because you're the only white guy here and they don't trust you, plus you're with a Hispanic woman."

That day expanded things for me. It shifted my view wider. What I would believe going forward is that there was a much wider world out there and God reaches us in different ways, but we still had the same destination in mind. I needed that shock to my system. It was a mundane activity, just walking around that mall, but still an eye-opening one because I was outside the world I grew up in, something that a lot of people don't get to experience.

My wife is also more liberal leaning than I, and she has been a blessing in opening my eyes to the plight of others. By the time I was in my early 30s my staunch conservative views began to change. This was also due to more maturity and my own study of the Bible. My dad planted the seed of my faith, but my former pastor, Daron Earlewine, tended the vine as I aged into my 30s. He was the one that really challenged me to get into the Word and make up my own mind about it. He is an amazing preacher and always

What I Believe In (and Why I Believe It)

challenges those listening to him to dig deeper and build on their own faith aside from simply trusting a pastor to do it for them. He was always big on saying "Open the Bible and read it for yourself. Don't just trust me."[1]

Daron was incredibly influential in helping me see that the Bible speaks to each of us differently. From there, the Word spoke to me about having care and compassion over strict obedience. His teaching showed me that making up my own mind about what I read is fine.

In my 30s there were two major events that greatly shaped my faith. The first was becoming a father in 2013. The day my son was born was the greatest day of my life. As the nurses were cleaning him up, I spoke to him and he looked at me, barely five minutes old, as if he knew me. His eyes connected with me like nothing ever has before or since. That moment shook me. I was now going to be responsible for guiding a life from birth. It was going to be my most difficult responsibility, but also my most rewarding.

I admit that I have not been perfect. In fact, I have made some large mistakes as a dad. Still, being a father has taught me grace. It has shaken my belief that I have to be perfect at all times because a child has infinite grace. That is what Christ has for us as well. My faith deepened because my son has shown me my imperfections in stark detail, yet I am still loved by him.

It is the same love Christ has for us. We are never going to measure up, but we are merely asked to have faith. He takes care of the rest. Now in my 40s, I finally feel grace for my transgressions. The Bible teaches forgiveness and Christ is the mediator for us in that department, but being a father finally allowed me to have grace for myself.

While my son has magnified my faith, the election of Donald Trump was an event that greatly shook my faith. I grew up during the heart of the Clinton Presidency. I was raised to think he was pretty much one of the worst human beings alive because he cheated on his wife. Remember how I mentioned I saw everything in black and white as a teenager? Well, it was magnified tenfold with him. The mentors I looked up to who helped establish my faith derided him, so I did to.

Now fast forward 20 years. The same mentors that I grew up with now celebrated a man whose personal life was much more open and ribald than Clinton's ever was. Trump was hailed as a great savior for "traditional Christian values" all while having a personal life that was well documented and far worse than Clinton's. It just did not fit with me. How was a twice divorced serial philanderer who had never shown remorse for his actions

---

1. Daron Earlewine—https://www.daronearlewine.com/

Compassion

somehow a great champion for the Evangelical cause? I am still no supporter of the Clinton family, but to me, Trump was the antithesis of every value I was taught to uphold, and those that were suddenly supporting him were doing so out of a betrayal of the very values they taught me. These same people that once vilified Bill Clinton for doing pretty much the exact same things Trump has been well documented as doing (and has even bragged about), was now "Chosen by God" to defend American Christianity.

It is a difficult path to walk. On the one hand, I find this view entirely hypocritical and the old black and white me wants to vehemently call them out on it. On the other hand, the maturity I have gained knows that this attitude does not exhibit compassion. This does not examine the *why* they believe this. After all, If I am supposed to know what I believe in and why I believe it, don't they, as well?

I admit that knowing where this belief comes from makes it even more difficult to come to terms with it compassionately. The church I grew up in believed that marriage was sacred, you should stay sexually pure until marriage, homosexuality was a terrible sin, abortion was evil, and women should be submissive to their husbands. They pull these beliefs out of the Bible because yes, they are in there:

- **Marriage as Sacred**—"Therefore a man shall leave his father and his mother and hold fast to his wife, and they shall become one flesh."—Genesis 2:24
- **Staying Sexually Pure**—"Let marriage be held in honor among all, and let the marriage bed be undefiled, for God will judge the sexually immoral and adulterous."—Hebrews 13:4
- **Homosexuality as a Sin**—"You shall not lie with a male as with a woman; it is an abomination."—Leviticus 18:22
- **Abortion is Wrong**—"You shall not murder."—Exodus 20:13
- **Women Should be Submissive**—"For the husband is the head of the wife even as Christ is the head of the church, his body, and is himself its Savior."—Ephesians 5:23

All of those are very familiar to me. They are basically words that were to be obeyed without question. As I mentioned earlier, however, being challenged to read and discover what the Word really says is important. The Christian writer Rachel Held Evans provided one of the best descriptions of the Bible I have ever read in her book *Inspired*:

What I Believe In (and Why I Believe It)

"The Bible isn't some Magic 8 Ball you can consult when deciding whether to take a job or break up with a guy, nor is it a position paper elucidating God's opinion on various social, theological, and political issues. While we may wish for a clear, perspicuous text, that's not what God gave us. Instead, God gave us a cacophony of voices and perspectives, all in conversation with one another, representing the breadth and depth of the human experience in all its complexities and contradictions."[2]

One definite thing I have learned in my study of the Bible is that you can pretty much find something that is going to support one side of a position or the other. Let's revisit those five points from above and see what the Bible has to say elsewhere about them:

- **Marriage as Sacred**—And Jacob did so. He finished the week with Leah, and then Laban gave him his daughter Rachel to be his wife. ^{29} Laban gave his servant Bilhah to his daughter Rachel as her attendant. ^{30} Jacob made love to Rachel also, and his love for Rachel was greater than his love for Leah. And he worked for Laban another seven years.—Genesis 29:28–30

- **Staying Sexually Pure**—Then David sent messengers to get her. She came to him, and he slept with her. (Now she was purifying herself from her monthly uncleanness.) Then she went back home. ^{5} The woman conceived and sent word to David, saying, "I am pregnant."—2 Samuel 11:4–5

- **Homosexuality as a Sin**—I grieve for you, Jonathan my brother; you were very dear to me. Your love for me was wonderful, more wonderful than that of women. 2 Samuel 1:26

- **Abortion is Wrong**—At that time Menahem sacked Tiphsah and all who were in it and its territory from Tirzah on, because they did not open it to him. Therefore, he sacked it, and he ripped open all the women in it who were pregnant.—2 Kings 15:16

- **Women Should be Submissive**—Now Deborah, a prophet, the wife of Lappidoth, was leading Israel at that time. ^{5} She held court under the Palm of Deborah between Ramah and Bethel in the hill country of Ephraim, and the Israelites went up to her to have their disputes decided.—Judges 4:4–5

2. Held Evans, Rachel—*Inspired: Slaying Giants, Walking on Water, and Loving the Bible Again,* Thomas Nelson, Inc., 2018.

Compassion

The Bible has plenty of examples of strong women who did not submit. There is plenty of allusion that the relationship between David and Jonathan may have been sexual. Dozens of men had multiple wives throughout Scripture. Sexual purity of every character is not a common trait. Children are righteously slaughtered throughout the Old Testament. It really is quite a book, and that is before you even consider that it was written over thousands of years, by dozens of authors, with the context of their time and circumstances (such as the Babylonian exile) clouding many of the pages.

Does that take away from its sanctity? Absolutely not! What it does do is allow us to view it in a different light when we're willing to step back from it. Rachel Held Evans also summed this up in later pages when she said:

> "God gave us an inspired library of diverse writings, rooted in a variety of contexts, that have stood the test of time, precisely because, together, they avoid simplistic answers to complex problems. It's almost as though God trusts us to approach them with wisdom, to use discernment as we read and interpret, and to remain open to other points of view."[3]

While I see many of the people that taught me the values I hold dear now violating said values in support of a man that is the antithesis of said values and it makes me very angry, I also see that they come to their position out of their own beliefs and lived experiences. Their point of view is different than my own. I fear their alliance is one against Biblical principle, as they are using him to seek political power from which they can enforce their beliefs on others, and he is using them for his own personal gain without caring a whit about anyone but himself. Evangelist Beth Moore made a great point about this recently on her Twitter feed when she said,

> "But what has become startlingly clear to me in recent years is that our interpretations can have a whole lot more to do with our agendas than our faithful exegesis. AND that sometimes secondary matters shift into primary matters because the gatekeepers fear a loss of control."[4]

Like the Pharisees, they fear losing their power. There is almost a fear there that seeing a different point of view is to be avoided, even if it means compromising the beliefs they say they champion. What they have is a

---

3. Held Evans, Rachel, *Inspired: Slaying Giants, Walking on Water, and Loving the Bible Again,* Thomas Nelson, Inc., 2018.

4. Beth Moore, @BethMooreLPM, https://twitter.com/BethMooreLPM/status/1486020385262948354

What I Believe In (and Why I Believe It)

marriage of convenience. Trump parrots what they want to hear so he can stay in power, and they use him to maintain complete influence and control at any cost. Never mind that control is an illusion.

As much as the humanity in me wants to shame them, at the same time I know I am called to love with compassion from the same book they champion. There are many people that believe that Donald Trump was chosen by God to be this nation's leader. You might be surprised, therefore, to hear me say that I, too, believe that Donald Trump was chosen by God. I believe it was as a judgement for a church that has lost its way by seeking power over compassion though. They are seeing the church shrink because people see what they view as hypocrisy and don't want to be a part of it. I am not surprised that church attendance is shrinking because people see that Evangelicals have such a devotion to supporting Donald Trump and they don't want to be part of it. They see it how I see it: that he represents everything antithetical to "traditional Christian values".

A report from Peter Wehner in The Atlantic outlines this corrupt bargain:

> "In judging how each side sees the relationship, let's start with the president. A man whose lifestyle is more closely aligned with hedonism than with Christianity, Trump clearly sees white evangelicals as a means to an end, people to be used, suckers to be played. He had absolutely no interest in evangelicals before his entry into politics and he will have absolutely no interest in them after his exit. In fact, it's hard to imagine a person who has less affinity for authentic Christianity—for the teachings of Jesus, from the Sermon on the Mount to the parable of the Good Samaritan—than Donald Trump.
>
> The less gullible or more cynical evangelicals view Trump transactionally. Trump may be using evangelicals to advance his aims, but they are also using Trump to advance their aims. (Many evangelicals have grown enamored with Trump's relentless attacks and aggression, believing that he is inflicting wounds on those who deserve to be wounded.) The president might not be a model Christian in his personal life, they admit, but he delivers what they want, which is power and influence."[5]

I struggle with my anger at this. It feels like a betrayal. As a hothead, my first reaction is to rail against this perceived hypocrisy and rub the

---

5. Wehner, Peter—*The Evangelical Movement's Bad Bargain*—https://www.theatlantic.com/ideas/archive/2020/10/the-evangelical-movements-bad-bargain/616760/

Compassion

offending party's nose in it. As Bryan Zahnd points out in his book "When Everything's on Fire", this can be counterproductive:

> "An angry reaction to *everything* in your inherited tradition is probably unwise and unnecessary. You may not need to take a wrecking ball to your entire theological house. Try to move in response to light and love and not in response to anger and resentment. Unless you come from an aberrant or abusive sect, you probably received many treasures from your tradition that are worth cherishing. They may have given you a bad eschatology or an ugly theology of final judgment, but they also told you about the Jesus that forgives sinners and offers abundant life."[6]

It is natural to feel this anger because those treasures, which are immeasurable, come from people that appear to have turned their backs on those values. It is difficult to reconcile this because I value the lessons and morals I learned under their tutelage so much, but at the same time their current actions have caused me to lose a lot of respect for them. The anger and frustration is only a natural reaction.

But the good news is that we can have compassion again. We are called to it. It was central to Christ's message, and it can overcome a lot of the evils that each side sees if we surrender to it. It is the lessons that we have learned that are so important. They provide a foundation for this compassion. They are the strength we draw upon to find a path for reconciliation in this world.

It's going to get uncomfortable here, but that's a good thing. Everyone needs to have their beliefs challenged because from that challenge we grow. I honestly see the Evangelical movement in America to be severely lacking when it comes to compassion. It goes beyond their political devotions and into what we see with serious societal problems that remain unaddressed, ignored, or even dismissed entirely.

Climate change is real whether you believe in it or not. The COVID-19 pandemic is real whether you believe in it or not. Systemic racism is real whether you believe in it or not. Many in the Evangelical church scream that God is real whether we believe in him or not (have you seen any number of billboards along highways?), but they choose to ignore real, live issues where there is an enormous amount of evidence. They are issues where the first step alone is to have compassion for those affected. As I will touch on later, they are called to "Do Something", both by the current

---

6. Zahnd, Brian—*When Everything's on Fire*—InterVarsity Press

What I Believe In (and Why I Believe It)

circumstances and by Scripture. When that "Do Something" means they must sacrifice something, however, they balk.

Some may say that we should simply live in faith that God is in control, but God also gave us the wisdom to live in this world and accomplish great things with the knowledge He gives us. We are also told, quite clearly, to not be passive. Many deny climate change, but all the way back in Genesis mankind was given dominion to care for the planet (and we have done a lousy job of it). We also have the knowledge to do something about it, even if the will isn't there. The same is true with the pandemic. It is fine to have faith God will protect you, but part of that protection comes from using the scientific wisdom mankind has been blessed with to protect people through research, treatments, understanding of how viruses spread, vaccines, and more. Science and religion can work together because God blessed us with the knowledge to figure things out.

We are unfortunately living in a climate where your side has to be 100% right and the other 100% wrong at all times, and that is not how we make progress. I look again to Beth Moore, who said in a Tweet:

> "I'm going to be candid here. If more of the big Trump supporters I knew had been more willing to say they were appalled by some of his actions, I could have handled the mess better. Nuance is a normal human thought process. What seems far less normal to me is picking a side and you are on that side, with that side and 100% in agreement with that side no matter what happens. Seems to me the most valid constructive criticisms with the most potential for change come from within."[7]

I still don't think that simply acknowledging that actions are appalling, yet being okay with the mess they cause is nearly enough, but her larger point is the same. Admitting mistakes and accepting fault is not something American culture does well on either side. That takes a measure of humility (and humility will be a focus of a later chapter), one that escapes most people.

What we believe in produces strong feelings, and these feelings do not respond well to challenge. Challenging these things are important though. I was surprised to see this summed up so well in an article from Liberty University of all places written by Will Young:

---

7. Beth Moore on Twitter, August 16, 2021—https://twitter.com/BethMooreLPM/status/1427252609254141952

Compassion

> If you are hesitant to explore other belief systems because you figure it may change your mind and cause you to shift on your beliefs, then I would question if you ever believed those things in the first place. God gave humans the amazing ability to reason, and that gift is going to the curbside by ever believing in something without reason in the first place."[8]

Talk about challenging a belief! I never thought something that thought provoking (nearly scandalous, considering the source) would come out of Liberty University of all places, but that is because my own beliefs about Liberty University are very skewed. I am willing to be tested and challenged by it though. It helps us become more secure in what we believe in. How much easier would this pandemic have gone if both sides were willing to retreat a moment, examine the evidence that the other side was presenting, and reflect that, "You know, maybe they are right?" We could not come together and believe in the most basic scientific evidence in front of us or that science might be fluid as we acquire more evidence, and it has led to this. Even worse, science and evidence were dismissed not because it was science or evidence, but because it came from a source we did not like.

We can do so much better. Yes, it is important to know what we believe and why we believe in it, but at the same time, challenging those beliefs is not a bad thing. By challenging those beliefs, learning new things, and incorporating that knowledge in with our beliefs instead of rejecting that knowledge as automatically counter to our faith we can learn to be more compassionate.

---

8. Young, Will—Christians should challenge their beliefs for a deeper understanding of faith—*Liberty Champion*—https://www.liberty.edu/champion/2017/10/column-christians-should-challenge-their-beliefs-for-a-deeper-understanding-of-faith/

2

The Smallest Acts Have the Largest Effects

ONE OF THE LARGEST reasons I started writing about compassion is that I have long struggled to have it. That makes this entire work born out of going against the grain, but as you will see, it is important to be challenged. When I was a kid, I was told I had great aptitude towards math and science, but I wanted to work in sports media. I became a writer mostly because people told me I couldn't become a writer. It is with that attitude that that I wanted to investigate this larger problem of a lack of compassion at large. I have struggled with it, so why not turn into the face of it and confront it.

My struggles come from always having a black and white nature, as I mentioned in the introduction. I have often taken a stance and refused to concede any middle ground on a topic. In my early 20s I was especially recalcitrant about this. I once didn't speak with a very good friend of mine for over a year because something they did was 100% wrong in my eyes. In this situation he had been dating one girl but started seeing another without her knowledge. I took it upon myself to tell the offended party because "it was the right thing to do."

What did it accomplish though? In the long run, nothing. It is not like I saved a relationship or painted myself a hero. If anything, I strained a long-time friendship with not only him, but the entire group we were mutual friends with. This was just one instance, too. There are pictures where all my high school friends are in them, except I am missing because I was taking some self-righteous stand that I can't even remember right now. These small acts led to a bad attitude from myself that lasted for many years, all to the detriment of the relationships I had cultivated with people.

It was the actions of said friends that were also important though. It has been more than 20 years since those incidents, but these people are still my friends. Why is that? They had compassion towards me in my own stubbornness. Even as I was being a jackass and standing on self-inflated principles, they saw the gray that I did not. I may have tried to write some of them out of my life because I disagreed with their decisions or actions, but they never wrote me out of theirs.

Now that we are all in our early 40s, I look back on their actions and care for me with deep thanksgiving. Their acts of patience with me, the way they still cared and knew I was a better person than my actions showed, paid off. Yes, there are still old hurts there and I carry a lot of guilt for my actions, but their small acts of compassion helped shape me. After mending these relationships, I have been able to return the favor as well.

We may not see each other much in person anymore, but I carry their phone numbers with me and there is a great peace in knowing they are all a message away. We have shared the joy of being at each other's weddings, announcing the births of our children, celebrating in personal and professional accomplishments, and we have been there in mourning for deep personal losses of parents and other friends.

It has taken time (probably way too much time), but these people have taught me the value of being open-minded. They have taught me to look deeper into a situation and care for those involved. They are not the only ones that have done this, but I can honestly say that they are the ones who have planted the seeds that helped me grow into a better person. That continued growth is something we should all strive for.

Where do we see compassion today? It is often hard to detect in large, sweeping gestures. We have billionaires using their wealth on vanity pursuits into space while the workers they employ struggle to make ends meet. We have members of Congress on both sides more concerned with obstructing legislation that might actually help people for reasons that are often quite transparent (i.e., the other side supports it). Every day brings a new group of people screaming at another, and as a society I see this nation as myself when I was a teenager: everything is in black and white. It is either good and needs to be supported fully, or it is bad, and it must be banished

The Smallest Acts Have the Largest Effects

from this earth in fire and smoke. What needs to be banished in said fire and smoke depends on which side of the aisle you're on.

Compassion has to begin with small, deliberate actions. It must be intentional and hopefully become viral as a result. These acts might be one person helping another, or even simply seeing those acts from one person to another. That can provide desperately needed encouragement to a third party that sees it.

For as much of a cesspool that Twitter is, there is some good that comes from it. The account @DudespostingWs is a great follow because it provides such encouragement. It is, as it describes, "Dudes posting their W's," and it has more than 1 million followers. It can be silly ones like a tale about a guy who caught a fish with his bare hands or a heartwarming story about a father whose son was diagnosed with an "incurable" brain tumor 17 years ago at age 11, but the father was now delighted to see that child get married in the present day. These stories of tenderness and victory honestly get me through a world that is overwhelming. They provide hope that not all is lost.

Now imagine how God feels. He sees all of this. He KNOWS all of this. I cannot even remotely pretend to know the mind of God, but I do know He is in full control, and we have seen the fingerprints of his mercy and compassion throughout human history. I am convinced that His grace and mercy continue to this day, even if we don't see it.

Compassion begins when we put ourselves above others. The ultimate example of this, obviously, is Christ's sacrifice. He was God. He was all-powerful. He was all-knowing. He could have rolled into Jerusalem as a conquering hero and laid waste to the established government. In fact, that is what many in his day wanted Him to do. Like The Bride in the first Kill Bill film, many of his followers wanted Him to come strolling into Jerusalem and start cleaning house with the Romans like they were the Crazy 88. They were quite disappointed when He didn't which is why He was virtually alone at the Cross.

We saw none of that swift and terrible vengeance because it was not His nature. His nature was to put others before himself. This included the very will of God as he prayed in the garden that the burden be taken from Him. Later, when Peter committed actual violence against the Roman authorities by cutting off Malchus' ear, Jesus took the time to heal it even as he was being led away by the Roman authorities.

In America we are presented with the role of "warrior Jesus" that will take no business from anyone and will strike down his enemies with

Compassion

righteous fury. This view takes Jesus clearing out the temple and hyper-masculinizes it. That's the Jesus people want: the one that is going to do the work for them with violence and thunder. This is the only time we see this, however, because the rest of the time Jesus is the master servant. Look at all these examples:

- His very birth was foretold in glory, but came quietly in a manger, not in a palace.
- He was a refugee in Egypt, forced to flee the cruel earthly authorities of His day.
- It is generally believed he did not begin his public ministry until his 30s. That's a long time to be working as a simple carpenter in Nazareth.
- His parables had a constant theme of service, with the Good Samaritan being the prime example.
- At the Last Supper He served his disciples, not elevating Himself above them, but by taking the lowly job of washing their feet.
- When given the chance to be ruler of all the earth during His temptation in the desert He turned it down.

In His example we are not called to live without a self, but to give ourselves in love and humility. We must place ourselves above others, and it begins with small acts that have larger consequences.

Some of the most profound moments of my life have come from similar small acts where I felt like I was being used by God Himself as part of something larger. One of my hobbies is that I run a sports blog and write about the athletic teams for my alma mater, Purdue University. This began with me writing on Blogger back in 2006 as a hobby but evolved over the past 15 years to become a large website supported by Vox Media with a dedicated following. Each day I am overwhelmed that something I created grew into something people want to read and is a place where hundreds of fans can gather to talk about our teams.

I also view having this audience as a responsibility, and I try to do good with it in small gestures. Within the Vox Media network there used to be a website called Everyday Should Be Saturday. It has now evolved into a podcast called the Shutdown Fullcast, which bills itself as "The internet's ONLY college football podcast". The founder, Spencer Hall, used to work for a refugee resettlement organization in Atlanta called New American Pathways, and a few years ago he came up with what he calls the EDSBS Charity Bowl.

The Smallest Acts Have the Largest Effects

The premise of the Charity Bowl is simple: he asks for fans of college football teams to donate to New American Pathways in a dollar amount as a measure of spite for their rivals. For example: As a Purdue fan, Indiana University our rival, so one way I can donate is to give $74.42 in honors of Purdue's 74-42-6 lead in the all-time football series. Contributors can do a one-time donation or donate monthly for an entire year.

It started slow, raising a couple thousand dollars a year at first, but has since exploded to raise more than $825,000 in the span of a week in 2021[1]. It has become the largest fundraising effort for New American Pathways each year. Since we have a large Purdue audience, I encourage our readers to give each year and we regularly contribute a couple thousand dollars to that total. It humbles me every year. I am just an idiot college sportswriter given a voice and an audience. To be able to ask that audience to help even in a small way and combine our efforts with a bunch of other internet strangers to donate and aid refugees, all out of sports spite, is awe-inspiring to me.

All the credit goes to Spencer, Holly Anderson, Ryan Nanni, Jason Kirk, and New American Pathways for this, but it is driven by the small acts where people put themselves ahead of others. Yeah, $74.42 may not seem like much, but this past year had more than 5,500 individual donors. These are ripples that grew into a huge wave thanks to Spencer deciding to do something small, and it amazes me that I have a place that can not only be a small part of it, but magnify its impact by adding other small parts.

This is a prime example of how everything does not have to be a grand gesture to grow into a massive impact. Yes, it would be wonderful if Jeff Bezos decided to donate his entire fortune to a worthy cause. We can still have powerful, small moments in our lives that amplify into larger ones. It is up to us to be the example we want to see in others. The important thing is to be actionable and intentional. See where you can find those small moments even if it is something like a text of encouragement to a friend. Being able to lift others over ourselves is one of the first steps we can collectively do to get compassion back in society.

One thing I have said throughout the pandemic that the United States is the only country that could politicize a public health crisis, and that is what we have seen since it began in March 2020. This was "magically going to go away", while the other side screamed "these foolish actions will kill us all". Far too many churches were concerned about the "freedom to worship how and where we want" instead of helping the sick and dying. On the

---

1. 2021 EDSBS Charity Bowl grand total—https://twitter.com/newampaths/status/1384292471010521102

other side, far too many people were fine to dismiss those people as religious zealots who deserved to catch COVID and die. Neither side covered itself in compassion, and it has only gotten worse since as this continues to drag on (at least as of this writing) far longer than it should have.

This pandemic has been a showcase for a lack of compassion, and it is a showcase I would have certainly passed on if I were a contestant on the Price is Right. What continues to amaze me is that people of faith rely on, "well God is in control and because of that X isn't real," While failing to acknowledge that God gave mankind the gift of wisdom to figure these things out and take actionable steps. As far back as the Garden of Eden man was given dominion to care of the earth, yet climate change is not real because mankind has neglected that responsibility?

It also goes back to what Jesus Himself did. Tyler Huckabee made a great point in an article for *Relevant* magazine regarding vaccinations and some of the hesitancy many churches have had concerning it:

> "I've been thinking about the miracles of Jesus lately. Of the 37 recorded in the New Testament, 27 involve healing sick people. I wonder why that is. There are no shortage of signs and wonders Jesus could have done. Other ancient stories are full of gods turning into animals or defeating monsters. Jesus made people's bodies better."[2]

Getting vaccinated against COVID-19 is not the end all/be all to defeating it, but it is a tool that can be used, and it shows compassion for other people (along with masks and such). These are small acts that have a wider effect in the long run, but they are small acts that too many refuse to do out of their own selfishness for whatever reason they use to justify it. God created us to live in a society and part of living in that society is having compassion for others in it. Whether you personally believe something is real or not does not change the realities of a situation in the world.

These small acts also are measures of humility, which is a critical element of compassion. They are actionable steps that say, "yes, I am thinking of someone other than myself when I do this." At heart, the road to compassion and caring for others begins with humility and admitting that we are not the center of even our own story, let alone at the middle of the universe. There is no shame at all in saying, "hey, I should do something that will benefit others."

2. Huckabee, Tyler—Getting Vaccinated Is Loving Your Neighbor as Yourself—*Relevant Magazine*—https://www.relevantmagazine.com/current/nation/getting-vaccinated-is-loving-your-neighbor-as-yourself/

3

Humility and Death of the Self

I HAVE ALWAYS BEEN a very big sports fan. One doesn't start a sports blog and have it grow into what it has become today if you don't love sports. My wife loves sports too, and by extension, so does our son. When we plan family vacations we try to see if there is a new Major League Baseball stadium we haven't been to yet either in the city we're going to or on the way. As of this writing I only have seven of the current 30 MLB stadiums left to visit, and my son, who is eight, needs only 12 of the 30.

Having been around sports my entire life there are so many small lessons in humility there, and I view humility as the prime basis for compassion. As a fan, you enjoy the big plays. Jon Octeus dunking ruthlessly on Collin Hartman is a gif that brings never ending joy to the Purdue faithful. There's the moment of anticipation, the dunk itself, then the pose of dominance.

While those moments stand out, sports show us humility in their overall flow. I LOVE basketball, but I was cursed with being too short and not very good at the game. I was never going to be the player making the huge dunk to physically dominate the opponent or hit the big three with the game on the line. When I did play, my role was always a support role. I played at breakneck speed, diving after loose balls, getting position to rebound, setting screens, etc. I had some moments scoring and such, but I was very content to do the dirty work and the little things needed to help my team win.

Compassion

Humility starts with attitudes like that, and humility is probably the first and most important attribute of Christ that I see. Humility is the death of the self. It is putting the needs of others before yourself. The apostle Paul stated this in his letter to the Philippians 2:3, saying, "Do nothing from selfish ambition or conceit, but in humility count others more significant than yourselves."

There is a certain fear that submission in one area means submission in all areas. The loudest refusals to submit seem to come from those that have never faced a single minute of real oppression or persecution in their entire lives. To them, even the smallest sacrifice for the common good, such as basic health measures during a global pandemic, is a step towards jackbooted thugs kicking down doors and openly persecuting them in the streets. It is not a surrendering of your rights to put yourself above others.

How can you view the life of Jesus and not see submission to the common good from the very beginning? Jesus was God in human form. He wasn't born into royalty. He did not pursue earthly power. In the same week that he entered Jerusalem with his followers salivating for him to take the throne and seize the means of power He humbly washed the feet of His disciples. If anyone in human history ever had a right to say, "I will not submit", it was Jesus, yet submission was the heart of his ministry.

When we look at the Bible, we have two ways of viewing things: A Christ-centered worldview and a Biblical-centered worldview. That statement can be a bit confusing when we do not know about one without the other, but let's try to unpack it a little.

Hebrews 12 says that Christ is "the author of perfecter of our faith". He is the central tenet of the entire Christian faith. Without Him, it means absolutely nothing. The Bible, however, is a little different. It was written over thousands of years, by several different authors, and is colored by the fingerprints of the men and women who contributed to it. Yes, they were inspired by God, but they were also influenced by their culture, surroundings, experiences, and more. It is their interpretation of the events and experiences of their time we that we see.

Yes, the Bible is the inspired Word of God, but "inspired" is carrying a lot of weight there. "Inspired" is defined as "of extraordinary quality, as if arising from some external creative impulse." I believe God inspired me to write this, but my own life experiences, culture, and circumstances are going to deeply color that. Wouldn't that hold true for the authors of the

Humility and Death of the Self

Bible's 66 books, especially when they are all a disparate grouping of works across a long period of time?

The only section of the Bible in which we have multiple points of view is on the life of Jesus. Therefore, we can get a clearer view of what He said and did. Each account speaks of His humility. Each account attests to how He served others ahead of Himself. Each account, repeatedly, shows His compassion, grace, and desire to serve. A Biblical-centered view of things can lead to hundreds of interpretations and views on thousands of topics. It leads to the wealth of contradictions pointed out by Rachel Held Evans as mentioned in a previous chapter. A Christ-centered view is much more focused on the ideals He preached, and that includes applying them in daily life.

There is another very important area when it comes to humility: It means submitting to God that we cannot force His will. Sometimes it was a hard lesson, but I have learned that there is not a single thing I can do to influence the will of God. I cannot make Him answer prayer. I cannot make Him get revenge on those who have wronged me. I cannot hasten His return to smite those who deserve it. Once I did learn that lesson, however, it helped me increase my faith, rather than decrease it.

Many of the mentors I have grown up with are deeply invested in Evangelical prophesy. I knew about the End Times, the worst parts of Revelation, and all kinds of prophesies since I was a child. In my 20s I read all the Left Behind books and saw them as history written in advance (which is often said in those books). I have long been told that the Rapture was going to happen in my lifetime, and I needed to be ready. All I needed to do was look for the signs that it was coming, with Russia and Iran combining to attack Israel as the number one sign from Ezekiel 38 and 39.

Is God capable of doing that? Absolutely. He's God. He can do whatever He wants. History, however, is littered with accounts of people fully confident that Christ's return was coming any day now dating all the way back to Roman times. I see more of it today from the Evangelical church almost as a longing that it will take them from this broken and fallen world that is just waiting to oppress them, at least in their eyes. Their view of the Rapture comes off as a cosmic lifeboat, saving them from the terrors of this world, and they merely need to wait for it to come.

This view leads to signs everywhere. Civil unrest is a sign of "wars and rumors of wars". Calls for social justice and societal change is a sign of the eventual persecution and dissolving of the global church (never mind that it

Compassion

has lasted for over 2,000 years). New technologies are viewed as harbingers of the Mark of the Beast. Seriously. In my lifetime I have seen bar codes, credit cards, microchips, and now vaccines as the latest "Mark of the Beast".

One of the common themes in this is the belief that we are not of this world. It is an end game faith. We only live to get our reward in the end, and anything in this world is merely temporary. I struggle with this because, if the only thing that matters is that end game, why did Jesus come to earth and mire Himself in it? Yes, all of this can happen, and we can be whisked away in the "blink of an eye", but until that happens, we have no choice but to be part of this world, like it or not.

According to Bryan Zahnd in "When Everything Is On Fire" he talks about the damage this view has done:

> "I dream of a church that is at home in God's good world instead of huddled anxiously at the departure gate. The idea that the goal of the Christian life is to go to heaven in general, and Rapture theology in particular, has done incalculable damage to how millions of believers think about the future. The Christian eschatological hope is not to go to heaven but to bring heaven to earth. The blessed hope is not that we're going but that Christ is coming. The closing scene in the book of Revelation is a picture of heaven and earth reunited in holy matrimony—a promise that is in the process of becoming. Jesus Christ as set forth in Scripture is the Savior of the world—not the Savior of parts of people for another world. Christians who are correctly taught what the Bible proclaims from Genesis to Revelation should of all people lead the way in caring for God's good earth."[1]

Remember: A Christ-centered worldview is based on what He did, and I see a Christ that deeply involved himself in the world around Him. His ministry was small and personal. He defied the religious elite of His day. Instead of revolting against the political leadership He submitted to their punishment on the cross. There is more than enough evidence that Christ deeply invested Himself in this world, so we need to invest in it as well.

I often find myself at odds with what I have been taught in the past and what I have learned on my own as I studied the Bible. I still see Evangelical prophesy all around me in many forms, right up to some declaring that Donald Trump will get a second term, one way or another, because "prophets said he would." Were there some that said he would get elected in

---

1. Zahnd, Brian—*When Everything's on Fire*—InterVarsity Press

Humility and Death of the Self

the first place? Yes. Kim Clement and Jeremiah Johnson were among those that said he would even before he decided to run. We can't deny that yes, he did become President, for good or ill, so it looks like they were right.

The thing about prophesy is that everything seems fantastic when it comes true . . . until it doesn't come true. Many other prophets, and some new ones, insisted that he would get a second term. Some have even gone beyond January 20, 2021, when he was no longer President, and insist it is only a matter of time until he is reinstated for a wide variety of reasons from tampered voting machines to divine intervention. The complete lack of evidence of fraud, courts throwing out lawsuits for lack of merit, and the fact that it would be completely unconstitutional at this point to put him back in office can be ignored.

This has led to a dangerous time of disinformation and a lack of faith. On January 23, 2021, Dr. Michael L Brown, a Jewish believer in Jesus and minister, was a calm voice of reason regarding prophesy. He tweeted:

> "To every leader who prophesied that Trump would remain in the White House, this is not about you now. This is about the name of the Lord being mocked and His people left in confusion and disappointment. I urge you to put your focus there, not on your own ministry or reputation."[2]

Because Evangelical supporters continue to pursue paths that the election was stolen, they open themselves to the mockery that Dr. Brown alludes to. It borders on delusion at this point. Despite overwhelming evidence to the contrary, there is still a large community of people that truly believe the election was stolen, and the acceptance of this lie is further poisoning both America and the church.

Could God part the clouds and reinstate Trump any time He wanted? Absolutely. He's God. Dr. Brown raises a great point even as a Trump supporter. It is not about any prophesy gone wrong. It is about doing the work called for us. I said earlier in this book that I fully believe Trump was elected and chosen by God, but as a judgement on a church and a people that has lost its way. Dr. Brown is right. The name of the Lord is being mocked and people are confused, disappointed, and even angry. People are mocking the "crazy Christians" that refuse to admit they are wrong, despite an overwhelming amount of evidence. Even though Dr. Brown still supports Trump, I respect

---

2. Dr. Michael L. Brown on Twitter, January 23, 2021—https://twitter.com/drmichaellbrown/status/1353054744437084163?lang=bg

him for having the courage to say the right thing here, especially when there are few that are willing to do the same on his side.

Even worse, I fear that Evangelical support for Trump has caused great damage to the Gospel because no one wants to be associated with a movement that has sold its soul and compromised the values it professes to have in support of him. In a recent article with WOOD TV out of Grand Rapids, Michigan Michael Guker, the president of the Collossian Forum summed this up well:

> "I think there are serious danger signs we need to pay attention to," he said. "For instance, the next generation is not particularly interested in churches that mimic the political ideology of the day because there's nothing interesting in it. You can go to your news channel. You don't have to go to church for that."
>
> In 2016, the Public Religious Research Institute reported 39% of young adults said they had no religious affiliation. That's up from 10% in 1986."[3]

It is true that there is an echo chamber. It applies both ways. Secular sources and their own agendas have hijacked the church and used it to advance what they believe in; not what Jesus spoke about. When Charlie Kirk speaking at a church is more welcomed and gets more agreement than the church's own pastor, that is a capital "P" Problem. It is driving people away from the message instead of bringing them closer to it. It is putting a man, Kirk in this case, ahead of the message because he is going to say the things that congregation wants to hear instead of what is needs to hear.

In the same article pastor Keith Mannes described why he left his church in October 2020:

> "I deeply loved the people I served and I was greatly blessed by them. But some large portion of the Church, broadly, had distorted and abandoned the message of Jesus and used it as a weapon to elevate an evil person in order to advance an earthly, materialistic, militaristic, selfish and anti-Jesus approach to humanity," said Keith Mannes, who gave his final sermon in October 2020 after four years of service to a Christian Reformed Church in Allegan County."[4]

3. Samples, Susan—Under God, Divisible: Political conflict deepens rift among Christians—https://www.woodtv.com/news/target-8/under-god-divisible-political-conflict-deepens-rift-among-christians/

4. Samples, Susan—Under God, Divisible: Political conflict deepens rift among Christians—https://www.woodtv.com/news/target-8/under-god-divisible-political-conflict-deepens-rift-among-christians/

Humility and Death of the Self

This is especially true because the words and actions of Jesus are right there. They can be read for themselves, and people can make up their own minds. Despite an overwhelming amount of real-world evidence, he still maintains broad support among Evangelicals, and that is deeply disturbing.

It is very, very plain that much of what Trump says and does is completely antithetical to what Christ preached. They handwash it though because they are afraid to lose political power to any one of several imagined fears regarding social change. Even worse, he has been elevated to near prophetic status in the eyes of many and is happy to revel in it by proclaiming "I am the chosen one!" Trump is more than happy to play on that and use them to maintain power. Imagine the howling and gnashing of teeth if pretty much any other political figure said that, yet it comes from a twice-divorced serial philanderer and narcissistic liar that is the antithesis of everything they profess to hold dear.

Even in all that, I am still called to have compassion not only for his followers that are plunging this nation down a very dangerous road, but to Trump himself because he is still a child of God. I can dislike and even abhor much of what he does, but I also have a certain sadness that he never received the lessons he needed to learn just to be a good person and that his followers continue to be blinded by his lies. I must have compassion and patience with these people because it is what I am called to do.

It comes back to that humility and submission to God. I have learned to accept a strong "no" from God on several prayers and accept that He is fully in control, while I am not. So far, at least, my prayers that people will have their eyes opened have been answered with a "no", but I must trust it is part of something larger.

Everyone gets a "no" from time to time. It is what we do with that "no" that shapes us. I continue to get a "no" for my prayers that there will be justice and actual consequences for those perpetuating this terrible regime. His supporters continue to get a "no" because he is not back in office. It takes humility to look beyond this frustration, see the situation as it is now, and to move forward.

I want to see Purdue play in A Final Four before I die, but for some reason God made Kihei Clark find Mamadi Diakite as time expired in the 2019 South Regional Final as I sat courtside and was a second or two away from seeing it in person, breaking my heart in the process. In the grand scheme of things, that is a very tiny no, but I have had some very large no's

Compassion

that were deeply personal and stung for years. They still taught me large lessons I needed to learn.

We must submit that sometimes God says no. He said no when I prayed Trump would not get elected in 2016 (and I was by no means a Hillary Clinton supporter), and he said no to others when he didn't get elected in 2020. There was no fraud, no hacking, and no conspiracy. He just lost, and God has another idea. Could the prophesy be true, and he gets elected again in 2024? Yeah, it could (though I really hope it is not). In both circumstances we as a society at large would greatly benefit from taking that Christ-centered view, really committing ourselves to doing the things Christ did, and doing those things on a small scale to hopefully ripple outward to larger change.

God is more than capable of handling the rest. If the End Times are real, they will come on His time, not ours, no matter what we do. We cannot force them to come or delay them no matter how much we would want to.

We can only affect the small circle around us. We are incredibly small in God's plan, but we are still asked to humbly submit and lose ourselves for the sake others. God's got the universe on His watch, and I am glad for it, because my simple human brain cannot even begin to fathom what running it is like.

The ultimate act of faith is living a Christ-centered worldview, doing what He did, living in the small moments, and getting out of the way so God can do the rest.

4

Being Selfish and Selfless with Grace

IT'S TIME FOR SOME whiplash. The last chapter was about the death of being selfish through humility. In this chapter I am going to encourage you to be selfish, because there is never such a thing as too much grace. Tullian Tchividjian is one of the many grandsons of famed Evangelist Billy Graham. Some of his best works are *Jesus + Nothing =Everything* and *One Way Love: Inexhaustible Grace for an Exhausted World*. The primacy of the infinite grace of Jesus has long been a central part of his ministry. That is with good reason, too.

Tullian is a bit of a black sheep when it comes to the famous Graham family. As a late teen he described himself as "dropping out, having a rebellion, and sinking into South Florida's 'pleasure saturated culture'"[1]. As someone with family in the Miami area I am very familiar with seeing the pleasure saturated culture of South Florida. It practically smacks you when you get off the plane. Even though he came back to his faith in his early 20s he has always been very different than his family.

He eventually became the pastor of Coral Ridge Presbyterian Church in Fort Lauderdale in 2008, where his style of preaching the Gospel came to the forefront. He was brought in to revive a church that had an aging population, but he drew the ire of elders by refusing to engage in the culture

---

1. Davis, James D.—Coral Ridge Presbyterian Church Chooses Pastor—*South Florida Sun-Sentinel*—https://web.archive.org/web/20090120032300/http://www.sun-sentinel.com/news/local/breakingnews/sfl-coralridge0118,0,7957788.story

Compassion

wars that saturate much of the Evangelical community. He shook things up. He didn't ascribe to traditional hymns and methods of teaching. He made people uncomfortable. Perhaps even more galling, he preached for <gasp> *change inside the church among Christians.*

Few people like change or challenges to their faith, but challenges can be a very good thing. What was Christ's ministry if not a change and challenge to the religious leaders of His day? I have often said that part of the struggles the Pharisees had was that they viewed Jesus as not quite the Messiah they were looking for. He shook them up, challenged their authority, and had the audacity to present a different way. Jesus threatened their hierarchy, so they decided to crucify Him for it.

This is why I like Tullian, because he challenged people to examine their faith and maybe even make a change, all in the name of grace. He preaches that grace needs to be *infinite*, and the ultimate test was when he resigned from his position in 2015 after admitting to an extramarital affair. A few months later he was fired from a non-pastoral position at Willow Creek Church in Winter Springs, Florida after disclosing a second affair. Here is what he had to say about grace after these events:

> "Until we see how bad we are, we will never see how good God is. Grace will become nothing more than white noise to us until we see how desperately we need it."[2]

Read that again: *Grace will become nothing more than white noise to us until we see how desperately we need it.* That is such a powerful message. Look at one of the largest "controversies" we see today in "cancel culture". Those that commit some terrible things cry out that they are the victims when they are held accountable for their mistakes (often because they have never been held accountable). The aggrieved insist upon a total shunning from civilized society for the aggressors. Where is the grace in this? As Jesus said, "But I tell you, do not resist an evil person. If anyone slaps you on the right cheek, turn to them the other cheek also. (Matthew 5:39)." Forgiveness and grace were central to his message.

Unfortunately, having grace is not in human nature. We naturally want vengeance. We also never want to admit when we are wrong. Many are trained that an admission of wrong is a sign of weakness. It takes humility to admit you are wrong. No one likes it, but a refusal to admit when we

---

2. Yap, Timothy—Year After Affair Admission, Divorce, Tullian Tchividjian Emerges With New Wife—*JubilieeCast*—https://jubileecast.com/articles/16451/20161129/year-after-affair-admission-divorce-tullian-tchividjian-emerges-with-new-wife.htm

are wrong often does more damage than good. It fosters a toxic culture, leads to mistrust, and undermines anything else we say going forward.

"For it is by grace you have been saved, through faith—and this is not from yourselves, it is the gift of God (Ephesians 2:8)" This grace comes not from Christ, but from the very heart of God. The Sacrifice on the cross was the act, but the grace itself comes from God providing that transaction through His Son. God became man and provided the grace for us because our nature is imperfect and flawed, making us incapable of mediating for ourselves. God didn't have to do it. That is the message.

In a recent blog post Tullian Tchividjian brilliantly summed up grace in relation to cancel culture:

> "Maybe this is the reason why Jesus himself was canceled by his culture and ours. The scandal of his promiscuous love toward those who are hated—his amazing grace to those who are guilty—is just too vulgar for a culture that has to find some solace in dealing with the uncomfortable log in their own eye by pointing out the speck in someone else's."[3]

To me, Tullian knows that search for grace the best. He has been very raw and up front about his personal failures in the last five years. His failures led to him being shunned by the larger church community because he was "unfit for ministry". He paid a price, and he knows it. His continual message is, "I broke my marriage, myself, and everything I stood for." He is very up front about both his actions and the consequences for them. Even then, he is still viewed as a failure by many. Ironically, he is viewed this way, even as he has been open and up front with both his mistakes and in seeking that grace from God, while others that are in a much larger light have not faced up to the consequences of their actions, yet they are forgiven. That still has not stopped him from starting an unaffiliated church that preaches grace and forgiveness. He still puts that message of grace ahead of everything, so who cares if he has a larger formal backing?

Such is the call for servanthood. Such is the call that the Gospel will not be stopped.

There is no such thing as being too unselfish or selfish with grace. This applies as much to our personal relationships as to ourselves. In fact, it may mean more when it comes to ourselves because we are our own harshest critics.

3. Tchividjian, Tullian—Jesus and Cancel Culture—https://www.tullian.net/articles/jesus-and-cancel-culture

Compassion

My grandparents on my dad's side divorced long before I was born, and my grandmother held a grudge towards my grandfather for DECADES before she passed away in 2015. In the 36 years I was on earth with her I might have seen the two of them in the same room three times, and one was for the funeral for my aunt in 2011. At one point one was living in Maine, the other in Hawaii, and my dad described it as, "a pretty good distance between them". I loved my grandmother very much and she was a good woman, but grace was not one of her strongest suits.

There was still some beauty in this. When she passed away my grandfather got in the car and drove to Indiana from South Carolina for her funeral. She never had a kind word to say about him, but he was still there, and even cordially spoke with my step grandfather at length, because there was once a relationship there. Both men had loved this woman. Their past did not matter that day. He still respected her enough that he wanted to come and pay her respects despite the many, many years of enmity between them. At the time I joked to my wife that I knew she was really gone because she didn't sit upright in the coffin the moment he walked in, but it was such a lesson in grace that he was there despite everything. It was an incredibly unselfish.

The selfish nature of grace is when it comes to forgiving ourselves, but this is one of the most difficult lessons to learn. I still try to hold myself accountable for my own mistakes, and I used to be worse about it. When I was at my darkest, I would hold myself in bitter disregard even with others selflessly forgave me because, "if I don't hold myself accountable, no one will." I had to always remember my own mistakes and failures, lest they be repeated.

I can tell you with great confidence, however, that this view accomplished nothing good. In fact, by not being selfish in grace towards myself I was committing an incredibly selfish act by drawing away from others. It did no favors in my marriage and led to some dark times with little joy, mild substance abuse, and self-isolation. It got so bad that I blamed myself for the mistakes of others because, "if I had been doing the right thing, their mistakes would not have happened."

See what kind of warped world view this is? If we don't have grace with ourselves first it is hard for others to have grace for us. In turn, we then struggle to have unselfish grace towards the others in our lives. Why would someone feel grace for us when we ourselves don't feel as if we deserve it? Worse yet, why would someone feel grace for us if we mire ourselves in such darkness that we don't accept it? Eventually they turn away because they don't want to see their own efforts bear little fruit.

I worked so hard to drive people away that once I came out of it, people I had driven away were gone. I had gotten what I wanted in driving people away, so the journey back to them would be lonely and difficult as I struggled to earn their trust and support again. In the end, it only made things worse, and I have found that I need to spend an equal amount of time if not more trying to undo that damage and find a way to earn the grace and trust of others. That can take years and is not a fun process.

I look at Peter though. Peter was an imperfect man. He was brash and said he would never leave Jesus, but mere hours later he was denying him three times. Jesus had infinite grace in forgiving him and making him the leader of the early church, but there still had to be a moment of personal forgiveness where he had to believe he was worthy of that grace. There still had to be that reconciliation after the Resurrection where Jesus personally went to Peter, forgave him, and made him the shepherd of His flock. As a result, we have the New Testament and the church exploded worldwide.

We need to have that kind of grace for ourselves. It is its own form of self-compassion. We need to be reckless with it, too. Grace towards ourselves leads to confidence, and with confidence we can accomplish great things. I wouldn't be writing these words if I didn't finally start to have grace for myself, and in early September 2021 I will cross the two-year milestone of when I finally made that huge step.

Grace is like air. We cannot survive without it and when we don't have it, things are quite suffocating.

In the book of Nehemiah you have an interesting picture that resonates with the present day. The story takes place in roughly the 5th century BC, and at the time, Jerusalem was in shambles. After the Babylonians had conquered Jerusalem, the Persians then conquered the Babylonians, essentially taking over for them. Nehemiah, the cupbearer for the king, asked to return to Jerusalem in order to help rebuild the city, and the king blessed his mission.

Upon returning, he found that the walls of the city were destroyed, so he began to work with local leaders to build up the city and repair the walls to defend against the enemies of the Jewish people. He was essentially in charge of the city with the king's blessing, so what he said, went.

As he was doing this, he discovered that the Jewish nobles were oppressing the poor:

Compassion

> Some time later many of the people, both men and women, began to complain against the other Jews. 2 Some said, "We have large families, we need grain to keep us alive."
>
> 3 Others said, "We have had to mortgage our fields and vineyards and houses to get enough grain to keep us from starving."
>
> 4 Still others said, "We had to borrow money to pay the royal tax on our fields and vineyards. 5 We are of the same race as the other Jews. Aren't our children just as good as theirs? But we have to make slaves of our children. Some of our daughters have already been sold as slaves. We are helpless because our fields and vineyards have been taken away from us."
>
> 6 When I heard their complaints, I grew angry 7 and decided to act. I denounced the leaders and officials of the people and told them, "You are oppressing your own relatives!"—Nehemiah 5-1-7

This angered Nehemiah, and he ended up cancelling all debts for the greater good of the people. This helped to rebuild Jerusalem, and for the 12 years he was in charge Nehemiah lived as an example by working more to repair the walls and by bringing the Jewish society together through shared resources. This was very much in line with many of the original principles of Jewish law laid out in Leviticus.

Where grace comes in is later in chapter 5. When confronted with their greed, Nehemiah was able to convince the nobles and officials to cancel debts and return property that had been mortgaged. Instead of seeking vengeance and punishment, the people came together as one nation. There was forgiveness of debts from those in charge, and forgiveness of oppression from those who suffered. That took an incredible amount of grace.

Nehemiah was essential in rebuilding Israel as a nation and returning it to the laws laid down by Moses. He separated it from its neighbors and repopulated the city after it had been decimated decades earlier. Eventually, the second temple was rebuilt, as Jewish society was brought back together.

This sounds very much like today, where wealth inequality throughout the world is a significant problem. Nehemiah is an example of someone who was given power yet was more concerned with the burdens the people had to bear than his own power and wealth. After returning to Persia those in Jerusalem fell back into their old habits, and Nehemiah had to enforce his reforms when he later came back.

There cannot be a resolution to the problems facing this nation without compassion and grace. Like in the time of Nehemiah, there must be agreement, and we are nowhere close to that if you pay even the most basic attention to the world. The rich are only getting richer, while those oppressed struggle to have their voices heard. I say this not because I have a magical solution, but to point out the importance of grace. Until we are willing to practice it, there will be no solutions.

This grace must be internal with our own communities too. We see communities torn apart because those that take a stand against wrongdoing within the community are cast out. Look at the case of Josh Duggar. Instead of facing actual punishment and consequences (which amounts to a measure of grace because it might result in tangible change) he was protected and coddled under the guise of "church discipline". As a result, his behavior was not changed, and he even took advantage of the grace he was offered. He made a bad situation worse because he was never called to show grace to those he had wronged.

Those that take a stand against wrongdoing should be supported instead of being cast out. Those that fear losing their power and go to all lengths, including ignoring things that are clearly wrong, should be corrected. It is going to take an enormous amount of work and grace, but it begins by listening and being open to compassion and change.

In her book "Living Brave" author Shannon Dingle uses the line "Grace is God saying 'Yes, this is yours, and I say you deserve it because it is mine to give.'"[4] If anyone deserves to withhold grace from people, it is her. Her story is both heartbreaking and inspiring. She was the victim of sex trafficking by her own family as a child and had a very dismal upbringing with all kinds of abuse. In college she met a wonderful man who loved her and accepted her in every way, making her feel safe. He was then killed in a freak accident while playing at the beach with their children in July 2019.

In the same book Shannon admits that she is mad at God, and she has every right to be. She still paints such a beautiful picture of grace with those words. I admire her so much for her rawness in the face of enormous personal tragedy. She could withhold grace from several people and even justifies why she has every right to do it throughout the book. She doesn't though. She is a living example of the grace we need not only for others, but for ourselves. In being open with her pain she strikes a chord with those that also struggle with burdens.

Throughout the book she often speaks of "allowing yourself to forgive yourself" and "allowing yourself to be imperfect." Her point seems to be

---

4. Dingle, Shannon—*Living Brave: Lessons from Hurt, Light the Way to Hope*—Harper Collins

Compassion

that we need to unselfishly have grace for others because of our imperfections, but we also need to be selfish with grace for ourselves. It is a great form of self-compassion that is difficult to even begin, let alone master.

5

The Duality of Being Grateful

"I'M FINALLY HOLDING ON to letting go."

In a book that is heavily based in Christian beliefs and teachings it seems out of place to use a song lyric from the band Slipknot. Their music is described as a "wall of sound" and is about as far from a church hymnal as you can get. Their song 'Unsainted' is a blistering 4 minute and 20 second track that I love to close my workouts with. The song itself builds into a crescendo where the lead singer shouts, "You've killed the saint in me!", and blasts into the final 40 seconds where each time I hit my closing kick with full ferocity.

I recently saw Slipknot as my first concert in a (somewhat) post-COVID world and they opened with "Unsainted". Maybe it is because I was in the middle of working on this when I saw them, but seeing it live made that lesson kick even harder. It became almost a spiritual experience because of the lesson that song taught me.

Aren't we all unsainted? John 14:6 says, "I am the way and the truth and the life. No one comes to the Father except through me." Romans 3:10 says, "As it is written: There is no one righteous, not even one." The metaphorical saint in us was killed with our own sin. Not only that, we also cannot possibly hope to regain that sainthood on our own. Only through the compassion of Christ and His sacrifice is there mediation. Thankfully, we don't have to do it ourselves because we would never measure up.

Compassion

Even the death of ourselves for humble servitude is not enough, because we are not perfect. We're going to screw up and make mistakes. We must have grace towards ourselves and let go of the vain hope that we can ever measure up, ever know the true heart of God, or even influence what He will do. We have to hold on to letting go of the baggage that holds us back.

It is more than the death of ourselves. It is the death of our egos and thinking we are the center of our world. If we are incapable of saving ourselves, what good is having the ego that we are at the center of the world? It continues Christ's consistent theme of submission, surrendering, and serving.

This song is a four minute and 20 second journey from beginning to end. It spins from the depths of despair to that strange ray of hope in, "I'm finally holding on to letting go." For years, I could not let go. I refused to forgive others, and even when I did, I refused to forgive myself because I was the architect of my own demise. I became mired in my own darkness, so much so that it became strangely comforting. An antidepressant I was on tamped my emotions down to the point I couldn't produce tears. I couldn't even cry at funerals for beloved lost family members during a 10-year period of my life. I didn't realize how numb I was.

In September 2019 I hit my lowest. I had long not been okay, but I was standing in my garage, drinking a beer in a particularly dark moment, and I looked at the rafters thinking, "What kind of Boy Scout are you? You couldn't even tie the knot." There was nothing actionable about it. I didn't come close to doing anything, but that low point scared me, especially since my family didn't know I was in the garage drinking a beer.

The hardest part was breaking through the complacency I had settled myself into and deciding to make a change. I had been on that antidepressant for roughly 10 years at that point. It had become a crutch. I was on it because I was convinced I needed to be on it, and I never tried anything different. I hadn't exactly covered myself in glory and brilliant decision making in that time, but in my mind, it was etched in stone: I had to be on it because any alternative was worse.

Have you ever been there? Complacency is a great place to hide because there is no risk. It happens to all of us: in jobs, in relationships, in hobbies. More than being challenged to read and think for ourselves in matters of faith, we must challenge ourselves in these areas as well. Yes, it is scary, but the benefit can be well worth the risk.

It has been more than two years since that moment with a lot of changes. I changed medication, and the nine-month transition off the old,

The Duality of Being Grateful

the trial of a new one failing, and moving to a third was its own deep hell. Around June, in the middle of the pandemic, no less, A fog finally lifted. I was finally clear-headed again. I finally felt free and could even acknowledge when things were going well. That last part was no small accomplishment, either.

In short, I was finally able to hold on to letting go regarding so much of my own personal baggage. It is still hard at times. My natural tendency is to slip back into the dark folds and wrap them around me like a warm blanket of misery. Never mind that this does not show any growth and strains every relationship in my life. It is an unfortunate coping mechanism that is difficult to overcome. Still, for the first time in a very long time I can see that I don't need that dark blanket of misery. I can have peace and even a measure of elusive rest.

I mention all this because it leads to gratefulness, which is yet another factor when it comes to compassion. It goes beyond merely being thankful. It is a deep feeling of peace that comes from perspective. I am grateful that I was finally able to see a new way to view things and allow myself to be imperfect. I am grateful that I can now admit when things are going well without fear that the mere mention that things are going well will reverse that trend.

I think there is a difference between being thankful and being grateful. Being thankful seems more rooted in the here and now. I am thankful for a hot cup of tea from the break room at work. I am thankful that the weather is nice and I can go for a run. Being grateful is different. I am grateful that I have a job that I both enjoy and is secure, especially when so many others do not have that luxury. I am grateful that I am healthy enough to be able to enjoy a nice run and hopefully extend my health as a result. I am grateful for a wife and son that have shone infinite grace in dealing with me as a flawed person.

Gratefulness comes from accepting the larger positives we receive in life and working to magnify them. To borrow from a sports metaphor, I am *thankful* that Wrigley Field exists, and I can visit it a few times a summer. I am *grateful* that the Cubs won the 2016 World Series because of the fandom passed on to me by my late grandfather. He created so many memories by spending time with me, watching the Cubs on WGN in the 80s. That was our time together, and when he took me to Wrigley for the first time in 1988 when I was 8 it was like getting a vision of heaven.

Compassion

Three years later, he would be gone, the victim of a massive heart attack. It is a loss I still feel more than 30 years later, but there is a gratefulness to that relationship, and it is extended to the Cubs. The Cubs helped to forge our bond. I was already a fan of the team, but that lingering bond magnified the entire experience. Good luck telling me to not cry now when I hear Eddie Vedder sing "Some Day They'll Go All The Way" at the end of the World Series recap video.

Being able to finally let go of my baggage and fondly remembering my grandfather even if he didn't live to see the Cubs win the World Series are just two examples of gratefulness, which is a key part of the compassion that we need for others. Compassion begins with us. The grace I focused on in the previous chapter is a step towards allowing ourselves to be grateful for the things and experiences in our lives. We can then allow that gratefulness to spill over into being compassionate for others.

There are numerous exhortations that say we should be grateful for God, but is He grateful for us? He really doesn't have need to be. He does not need humanity. In fact, there is a large portion of the Bible where he has either attempted to wipe out humanity (The Flood) or has plans to do so (Revelation). Remember though, the Bible is the *inspired* word of God, and it is impacted and colored by the lived experiences of the men and women that wrote each piece.

It is still central that we are grateful to our Creator, but I also think that He is grateful for us. The entire story of Jesus reflects that God is grateful for mankind because He became one of us. He is the mediator for us because we cannot mediate for ourselves. Jesus Himself gave thanks several times to God, and He was part God! He was also thankful for the disciples who continued His public ministry after His ascension.

I also think that God is grateful when we do the things that Christ asks us to do. This is not a substitute for his sacrifice, nor is it a way for us to gain salvation. We show our own gratefulness in living the example set before us, and in turn, God is grateful that we are aiding our fellow man. It becomes a reciprocal relationship then. We appreciate the sacrifice and show that in our works. God is then grateful because we see the need for Him and that we have joy in repaying it.

Think of it as the relationship between mentors and mentees. Before COVID 19 hit, when I was right in the middle of my own personal hell in changing medications as mentioned above. I was coaching my son's YMCA basketball team. It was a team of seven kids, ages 6–8, and we were not going to the NBA Finals that year. All of these kids had different abilities and skill levels. Some could dribble with speed and took to the drills with aplomb. Others could barely hold a basketball. Over the course of the program, they practiced and improved their skills. Even better, some of the kids that were shy started to come out of their shells.

Our team had one of the few girls in a league of mostly boys, but it was a joy to teach her and help her gain confidence with her dribbling and rebounding. After a few weeks she was outplaying many of the boys on the floor. It was a joy to see her confidence soar as the program went on. The first week was rough with a lot of individual play in our "games" with other teams, but by the end of the program we were the best team in the league because they learned to play together. It also helped that I emphasized no one player was above the other, even my own son, as I had to bench him for an entire game one week due to him getting in trouble at school and not following instructions.

Those kids were grateful to me because I took the time to work with them for an hour on Saturday mornings from January 2020 until the program ended about a week before the pandemic hit in full force. They were grateful that I could help them learn new skills, gain confidence, and meet new friends.

Conversely, I needed those kids to help me with what I was going through at the time. During my personal struggles, I looked forward to our Saturday mornings together. I needed their joy on making a basket. I needed to be out here, running up and down the floor and calling out instructions along with the coach on the other team. I needed their amazement in seeing that I could hit a shot from beyond the three-point line or even dunk a basketball on the goal lowered to 8 feet for them.

On my desk at work I have the team picture and it is just of me and those seven kids. I am standing in the back, towering at least a foot over all of them with my own son directly in front of me. I see it and fondly remember one of the most fulfilling things I have done in a long time, and I am immensely grateful for it. They did more for me than they will ever know, and I can see where God sees the same in us when we are compassionate towards others. All they did is stop and listen. We need to do the same.

"Give thanks in all circumstances; for this is God's will for you in Christ Jesus." This is from 1 Thessalonians 5:18, and it yet another reminder from the apostle Paul that we should take a posture of gratefulness in all things. I am aware that they seem like mere words. It is hard to take an attitude of gratefulness when all hell is breaking loose. When you lose a job, get diagnosed with an illness, lose a loved one, or anything like that, having an attitude of gratefulness is difficult. It can be overwhelming, and it can make you want to lash out at God.

It's okay to be mad at God. "The patience of Job" is an oft-used phrase, but even Job got mad at God. There are several other instances of Biblical characters being mad at God. Moses, David, and others had their own times where they were angry. The anger itself is not the problem. God can handle it. In fact, I think God is completely fine with it because our anger allows us to be honest with ourselves and our feelings if we examine it. It can be window to our souls and give us a moment of self-reflection.

I have been angry at God several times. It is usually because something did not work out the way I wanted it to work out. It has led to some intense prayer, which is fine, because I think God expects us to pray honestly. He doesn't want us to find the right flowery language that will unlock everything if we just say the magic words. It is not some Harry Potter spell. Once the anger subsides though it allows for moments of clarity. Was I mad about something not going my way? Well, maybe it was good that it didn't go my way because it was really a moment to learn. Was I angry because God gave me an obvious "no"? Well, maybe God had a "no" for a reason. As I mentioned previously, "no's" can always be a chance to learn and grow if we are open to that growth.

In a way, I am grateful for the ability to be angry with God. If we control our anger and not let it control us, we can grow, and I am grateful for that opportunity to grow. Even when that anger is born out of grief or loss it shows our humanity. Raw feelings are justified. They allow us to release things rather than keep them inside. This includes anger with God. He knows we're mad. Once again, He's God. He also wants us to use these moments to grow so we can be grateful later.

It is hard to speak on the mind of God and how He can be grateful for us because, again, I am not God. I know I say that a lot in here, but I base it in the humility of admitting I very easily could be wrong. I truly do think God is grateful for us. Even if you agree with me, you may think so for different reasons. I think we see it in His infinite patience with us because there are more than 7.5 billion people on the planet, all with unique hearts and desires, yet He is willing to meet us where we are, even if that meeting place happens to be in anger.

How is that not being grateful for us?

6

A Sam's Club-Sized God

How BIG DO YOU picture God? I see Him as the Creator of the universe. One of the most fascinating pictures in existence is from Voyager 1 on February 14, 1990. At that point the space probe had been traveling for 12 ½ years and was 6 billion kilometers from earth. It took a mosaic of 60 individual pictures that, when laid out, formed a "family portrait" of the solar system with Jupiter, Earth, Venus, Saturn, Uranus, Neptune, and the Sun (with Mercury too close to the Sun to be seen).

This picture is fascinating because it represents nearly the entirety of our Solar System, of which Earth is just a small part. Every human being that has ever existed was in a single frame of that 60 frame Mosaic, as Earth was represented as a pale blue dot that barely made up a single pixel. That was more than 30 years ago, and Voyager 1 has since become the first man-made object to officially reach interstellar space, leaving a solar system that is a mere tiny fraction of the universe.

And God is in control of all that.

Astronaut Michael Collins was in a unique position on July 20, 1969. As the sole occupant of the command module on Apollo 11, he was alone as it orbited the moon while Neil Armstrong and Buzz Aldrin were on the surface for nearly 24 hours. For 47 minutes of each orbit, he was on the dark side of the moon, and the physical body of earth's natural satellite blocked all radio communication with both Earth and Neil and Buzz on the surface. He was as utterly, truly alone as any human being has ever been,

Compassion

and only the other five astronauts (Dick Gordon, Stu Roosa, Al Worden, Ken Mattingly, and Ron Evans) who manned the command modules of the remaining five moon landings have experienced it. It was something that Collins was quite profound about:

> "I don't mean to deny a feeling of solitude. It is there, reinforced by the fact that radio contact with the Earth abruptly cuts off at the instant I disappear behind the moon, I am alone now, truly alone, and absolutely isolated from any known life. I am it. If a count were taken, the score would be three billion plus two over on the other side of the moon, and one plus God knows what on this side."[1]

He would later describe feeling, "awareness, anticipation, satisfaction, confidence, almost exultation". While he doesn't specifically mention meeting or talking to God in a "Hi, I'm God! You might remember me from such events as: The Creation," way, it still sounds like a deeply spiritual experience. Here is someone who stared into the face of all creation and was left in awe of it.

God is just that big, and it is yet another source of His compassion and caring.

I feat that too many people don't see God as being all that big anymore. I can only speak from a lived experience as an American in my 40s, but I see many out there that see God as way too small. They see Him as a God that can be easily defeated by the whims of mankind, and only True Defenders of the faith can prevent the world from falling into total anarchy where Christians are openly persecuted in the streets. Ironically, these are often the same people that would welcome the Rapture where . . . Christians are openly persecuted in the streets during the Tribulation.

It is one thing to believe in the tenets of the Bible and use them as a moral compass while seeing it as a message for salvation. It is something else to believe you or someone else is chosen by God to the point that even those rules don't apply. This is how we get "flawed men being used by God" as a way to hand wave away the character flaws that would otherwise be disqualifying. It also presents another example of a small God because it implies that His grand plans need our help, and even intervention, to come about. "If we just elevate the right guy, he will change everything to the perfect utopia and stave off the Rapture we desperately also want to happen."

---

1. Jacobs, Bob—Statement from Apollo 11 Astronaut Michael Collins—https://www.nasa.gov/home/hqnews/2009/jul/HQ_09-164_Collins_statement.html

A Sam's Club-Sized God

That certainly does not sound like a big God to me. It is terribly frustrating to see people like this with a voice who project a God that is so small and powerless. They project Satan going about "like a roaring lion (1 Peter 5:8)", but always seem to forget that Satan's power is insignificant next to the power and might of God.

There are even battles on if we should show compassion within the church. Look no further than the Bethlehem Baptist Church in Minneapolis. This church has been around for 150+ years and famously was led by John Piper for 31 years. Several members of the staff, including Piper's successor, have recently resigned over the way that some, especially Doug Wilson, view what they call "untethered empathy":

> "God commands us to be compassionate. He commands us to show sympathy, but people demand empathy, and they regard it as a kind of betrayal if you refuse to join them in their pain, in their grievance," he says in the series with Wilson. In this context of untethered empathy, he argues, "you lose the ability to actually make an independent judgement about anything that they're saying or doing. In other words, you lose contact with truth."[2]

Once again, I fear this is completely losing sight with what Christ taught us. John 11:33–35 speaks of Jesus joining people in their grief and being deeply moved by it, all without asking. It is ends with "Jesus wept". He didn't preach. He didn't coddle. He didn't "lose contact with the truth". He joined Mary and Martha in their grief. He didn't even have words for them. He was merely there, showing empathy. He was ready to listen and even join them in their pain.

Romans 12:15 asks us to "rejoice with those who rejoice and weep with those who weep." Again, this comes without reservation or conditions. Our very grace and the mediation that Christ does before the Father for us comes without conditions,

It is deeply saddening to see some advocating restrictions on empathy and compassion, even as I struggle with expressing empathy and compassion. It is my first instinct to dance and say, "well, it's your own fault. Deal with it," when I hear stories of people getting a big dose of reality, especially when their actions have caused harm elsewhere. We desire to see people face a comeuppance, and with my overwrought sense of justice, I admit

---

2. Shellnutt, Kate—Bethlehem Baptist Leaders Clash over 'Coddling' and 'Cancel Culture'—*Christianity Today*—https://www.christianitytoday.com/ct/2021/august-web-only/bethlehem-bcs-minneapolis-resign-meyer-empathy-rigney.html

that I have taken joy in the past when people face the consequences of their actions. It is easy to say, "well, you f***ed around, now you found out."

This is harmful, and it makes me no better than those that would put conditions on empathy and compassion. It is my own form of judging, which has carried its own warnings throughout the Bible. In placing limits on what I have empathy for just because I disagree with the person I should show it to, I am hypocritical in my own thoughts and actions. This goes completely against the infinite grace and patience that the big God I believe in shows with us.

There are struggles with believing in a big God. We see it in the trials of the world. Kids get cancer. Genocides happen. There is injustice rampant both around the world and at home. When we believe in a big God it is natural to question why things like this happen. It can cause us to have a smaller view of God, or even wonder if He exists at all (and yes, it is natural, and even okay to question if God exists). Ironically, it is in these moments that those I described above as having a small God seem to inflate their belief to a bigger God because "His ways are not our ways." It creates an interesting juxtaposition.

I don't know, and will likely never know, why God can be so big in some moments and so small in others. Honestly, anyone else who says they know is lying. We are all products of our own lived experiences, and these tinge our faith in unique ways so no two people have the same faith. That is something we must accept, and it is completely in line with the way the Bible was written. Other people's view of faith is completely different from our own. The authors of the Bible have a larger audience for what they believed and why they believed in it, but they were still shaped by the cultures of their day and by their own lived experiences. That had an enormous effect on what they wrote, especially when you consider they were writing from their time and not the present day.

Just look at the current state of the Christian church all over the world. There are hundreds of denominations. There have been hundreds more over the centuries that have risen up, then flamed out. Some denominations are slightly different from others while others differ wildly. Each has their own unique perspective and have been shaped not only by their founders, but by the current leadership they have.

The Catholic Church is currently the largest individual denomination in the U.S., representing 22.7% of the population. All Protestant denominations make up roughly 48.5% of the population, with the Southern Baptist

A Sam's Club-Sized God

Convention being the largest of those denominations at roughly 5.3% of the U.S. Population. Many of the Protestant denominations fall under the umbrella of "evangelical", which, depending on your definition, can make up close to 35% of the total population. I would identify myself as "evangelical", with the small "e" because of my own belief in Christ, but not "Evangelical" with the large "E" because of its connotations to the Conservative Right in America.

Yeah, it's complicated, but matters of faith can be complicated when we look at them closely.

The larger point is that we all serve a big God, even if there are gigantic discrepancies in how our faith is practiced. Given my background I would also likely be classified as an Exvangelical. I was raised in a very conservative environment (central Indiana) and used to have much more conservative social and political stances. As referenced earlier in this book though, what I learned in my study of the Bible and in other commentaries shaped my faith. Also, what I learned from other pastors, mentors, friends, and theologians had a significant effect on my current view. The current state of the world has also been a factor, and I suspect that until my time comes there will be other influences that make me stop and ponder that question I asked earlier in this book of, "What do I believe in and why do I believe it."

I still believe in Christ and in many of the tenets of Evangelicalism, but I can no longer reconcile them with the more overtly political nature of the modern Evangelical movement. It's still the same God and I must have compassion towards those mentors that planted those early seeds of faith, but I cannot agree with their actions that run against the values they profess to believe in.

In all this, I am reminded of one of my favorite movies. The film *Dogma* was written and directed by Kevin Smith. He grew up a very devout Catholic but, like me, saw his faith evolve as he grew older. He had a larger platform as a Hollywood director to address that evolution, and he chose to do that in making the film.

By most Christian standards the film is raunchy. It has Jay (Jason Mewes), a foul-mouthed drug dealer with his companion Silent Bob (Smith playing an on-screen role), who rarely speaks. Bethany (Linda Fiorentino) is a worker at an abortion clinic, yet a devout Catholic, who is "the Last Scion" as a descendant of Christ's mother, Mary. You also have Alan Rickman as the Voice of God (because if humans actually heard God speak their heads would explode), Chris Rock as Rufus (the 13th apostle, left out

Compassion

of the Bible because he was black), and Ben Affleck and Matt Damon as two angels, Bartleby and Loki, cast out of heaven by God (played by singer Alanis Morrisette).

There is A LOT that you will not find in a traditional church in this movie, but that is the beauty of Kevin Smith's filmmaking. In making a comedy that got the Catholic church to protest screenings of it he makes some very, VERY good points about faith. In a scene in the middle of movie Chris Rock's character talks on his experience of being an apostle with Jesus and faith as follows:

> "He still digs humanity, but it bothers Him to see the shit that gets carried out in His name—wars, bigotry, televangelism. But especially the factioning of all the religions. He said humanity took a good idea and, like always, built a belief structure on it."

This is in relation to an earlier line from the character Serendipity:

> "When are you people going to learn? It's not about who's right or wrong. No denomination's nailed it yet, and they never will because they're all too self-righteous to realize that it doesn't matter what you have faith in, just that you have faith. Your hearts are in the right place, but your brains need to wake up."[3]

Is it really that simple? Is it as easy as, "just have faith," when it comes to Christ? It seems like it could be simplified instead of having a lengthy list of rules and laws. Ryan Carrell, a pastor for The Southeast Project in Indianapolis, Indiana, had a great line in a sermon of his I listened to in a podcast. He said, "A faith bound up by rules & laws is not faith. It is just rules and laws."[4] Yes, the Bible is full of rules and laws. Just look at Leviticus. There are 613 laws put down in Leviticus. It is . . . extensive, to say the least. In Matthew, Jesus said that he came to fulfill the law, not to abolish it. He fulfills that law for us because we are unable to do so. We all fall short, so Christ, in His compassion, does the hard work for us.

That's what having a big, Sam's Club-sized God is like.

I fear that we lose sight of that big, Sam's Club-sized God when we bicker over the finer points of faith. The Bible is clear that Christ is all-embracing. His radical teachings involved communing with the less fortunate, promoting equality, eliminating poverty, healing the sick, turning the

---

3. Smith, Kevin—*Dogma*—View Askew Productions—Lions Gate Films—1999

4. Carrell, Ryan—Ephesians Sermon Series—https://www.wearesoutheast.org/ephesians, May 16, 2021

other cheek, hating money traders, and overthrowing oppressive systems. That is what is revolutionary. It is counter to so much of modern society, yet something that feels like common sense.

Unfortunately, humanity is corrupted by pride, greed, feelings of superiority, and more. It is heartbreaking to see, yet it makes those small moments that I talked about in Chapter 2 even more important. We have to live in those small moments and trust that a big God is going to do the things we cannot. We must trust that faith is individual. It is not one size fits all. What works for one person doesn't work for the next. When we put conditions on faith, we wander from the fact that we just need to *have* faith and that our own personal journeys are different.

Yes, we are to help others. Yes, we can be fellow travelers along similar paths of faith. Yes, we can even open the doors of faith for those that have either had none or who need a refresher that faith is possible. Their journey is still not the same as our own. I have been with my wife since we started dating in 2002. As of this writing, that is more than 19 years, yet her path is very different from my own. Her experiences before she met me are vastly different and they have influenced her own faith. To say that I know every answer to her questions and her personal relationship with God is the height of hubris. She is an incredibly intelligent woman blessed with numerous gifts that are different from mine. Her strengths are different from my own. If she has been given these things by The Creator, and they are different than what I have been given, why wouldn't her faith be different?

That is the beauty of such a big God. Can't you see it? We are all different, yet we are all equal in His eyes. We have all experienced different things, but He knows all those things individually. Our thoughts, our feelings, our daily lives, our fears, our triumphs, our sorrow, our intimate moments: all of these are unique. They set us apart, but there is still one God that is big enough to know ALL of it.

This is why I cannot get upset on a lot of "culture war" issues. If you're LGBTQ+, you're a person first and foremost. That's cool. I may not understand why you are that way, but I know I don't understand *because* I am not in your head and have not lived your experience. It is a foreign concept to me because my experience is different, but that's okay. I still view you as a human being because I expect people to see me as the same first and foremost.

Yes, we all carry labels. I am a father, a husband, a son. I am a man. These only define a part of who I am though. It is a matter of treating people

Compassion

with some basic human dignity regardless of their background or experiences because everyone's journey is different. There is no such thing as a one-size-fits-all map to life. That is why it is imperative to treat others with respect and see them as people first. They are fighting their own fights just as we fight our own. In doing so we show the heart of a big, Sam's Club-sized God.

7

Truth AND Consequences

IN THE PREVIOUS CHAPTER I mentioned having an overwrought sense of justice. That is probably understating it a bit. I believe in justice, being responsible for your own actions, and being held accountable to a fault. In this regard, I have always been ridiculously hard on myself, justifying it with an attitude of, "if no one else will, I need to be." I am sure my therapist really enjoys this aspect of my personality.

I was taught from an early age that I needed to be responsible for my own actions. No one else could make these decisions for me. I took this lesson to heart, so much so that it led to one of the few times I have stood up to my father in an argument. As an Eagle Scout I have long valued the Scouting tradition, and my dad was my Scoutmaster. We were in the car leaving a football game one day and he was upset about the Boy Scouts now allowing girls to be part of the organization and letting them take part in every activity. He said something to the effect of "teenage boys can't be trusted around teenage girls." He had even gone as far as saying he would no longer be involved in Scouting in any way because of it

At this point, I was upset because I deeply enjoyed my time in Scouting and it was one of the primary bonding activities we had, but suddenly it was not a great organization in his eyes because of its more modern policies. Also, I was once a teenage boy, so it is not like I was unaware of what it was like to be a teenage boy. It felt like he was throwing away a large part of my youth. I simply responded with, "well, I would imagine you teach them to be responsible for their actions, kind of like you did with me."

There was silence in the car the rest of the drive, but I can say my mother and my wife were suppressing smiles.

Life comes with consequences, and one of the most frustrating things for me is when people do not have to face consequences for their actions. I probably think this way because it was instilled in me early on that there would be consequences, and too many have never had to face any real consequences in their lives. An example is the case of Ethan Crouch.

In June of 2013 a 16-year-old Crouch was drunk and high while driving on a restricted license. He was speeding in a residential area when he collided with a group of people who were aiding a stalled vehicle. He ended up killing four people and injuring nine, one of them suffering complete paralysis. In what was a grievous injustice, he received a sentence of 10 years probation and therapy. His attorneys argued that his rich parents never gave him any boundaries, so he did not understand things such as consequences. This sums up what many people thought about the situation:

> "The case—and that portmanteau, "affluenza"—sparked national outrage. "It's disgusting!" Dr. Drew Pinsky told CNN's Anderson Cooper. "It's a cute, clever twist of a phrase that the psychologist should be ashamed of himself for having brought in the courtroom. And even more shameful is the judge for having fallen for that nonsense." This was the son of a well-off family escaping consequences by saying he'd always avoided consequences. It was proof of separate justice systems in this country, one for the rich and another for the poor, and Ethan became the face of wealth and privilege."[1]

Crouch was later the subject of an international manhunt and was arrested in Mexico because (surprise) he had violated the terms of his probation and was still partying. His mother even faced consequences for helping him evade authorities in Mexico. It is a tragic and infuriating case because even though he eventually spent two years in jail, he was still running afoul of the law as recently as 2020.[2]

---

1. Mooney, Michael J.—The Worst Parents Ever—*D Magazine*—https://www.dmagazine.com/publications/d-magazine/2015/may/affluenza-the-worst-parents-ever-ethan-couch/

2. Zarrell, Matt and Torres, Ella—'Affluenza teen' Ethan Crouch to be released as his lawyers argue testing will show he didn't violate parole—https://abcnews.go.com/US/affluenza-teen-ethan-couch-arrested-probation-violation/story?id=68036264

Truth AND Consequences

While it is easy to have compassion for Crouch's victims, it is much harder to have some for Crouch himself. What lesson has he learned? What real consequences did he have to face for his actions? It is maddening, but at the same time, I can see the door for compassion there simply because of his defense. Here is a young man that could have been so much more. He already entered the world with the benefit of generational wealth. He could have accomplished a lot of positives, but instead both of his parents failed him. By not providing him with guidance and wisdom he grew up believing he was special in the world and rules did not apply to him. His lack of any real legal consequences only affirmed this.

That is why consequences are born out of compassion. When I must deliver consequences to my son it is done out of love. I refuse to let him think that actions have no consequences, because that way lies a life like Ethan Crouch, even if it doesn't end up that dramatically wrong. My dad did the same with me. From early on, it was clear that there would be discipline.

I admit that I was very lucky and blessed growing up. My parents were not rich, but we were comfortable and without worry of where our next meal would come from or if we would have a roof over our head. They worked hard, and my sister and I benefitted. Discipline was still important though. As Hebrews 12:11 says, "For the moment all discipline seems painful rather than pleasant, but later it yields the peaceful fruit of righteousness to those who have been trained by it." The book of Proverbs is also steeped in lessons on discipline.

Due to my parents' hard work, I was very lucky and appreciative that they could pay for me to go to college. The day I moved in I was reminded that with that compassion and love came consequences if I strayed from their rules. After getting me set in my dorm room my dad turned to me and said, "Son, I'm happy to help you get your education, but if you quit, flunk out, get married, or have a kid I am taking it as a sign you're ready to be on your own and you will be."

On a related note, I graduated on time, completing an honors program, with a 3.4 GPA and could have even graduated a semester early if I had pushed.

I knew my father was deadly serious in his words that day. After he said them, he turned and walked out the door, and there was no question in my mind that I would face those consequences he mentioned if my actions dictated them. I am grateful for it though. There was compassion there because my parents were more than happy to provide me with opportunity and guidance, but at some point, I was going to have to make my own decisions and be ready to live with the result of them.

A large part of the bitterness (and yes, it is bitterness) I feel as an Exvangelical stems from a lack of consequences for those I have trusted, for those that continue to do wrong in the world, and by the fact that I struggle to have compassion for said people. It is hard to avoid being jaded when some scandal breaks in the news, yet there are zero consequences for the person involved regardless of the amount of evidence in their wrongdoing. I see stories like ones involving sexual assault in the church where victims are shamed for their alleged role while the aggressor either walks free or is placed under "church discipline". The case of Josh Duggar is an excellent example of this. He is a man with some very serious issues yet was allowed to walk at every opportunity instead of face real consequences, all while his victims (including his wife) were blamed for his behavior.

Where was the church's compassion there? Why were the victims at fault? It is related to the story in the previous chapter in how untethered empathy is suddenly a bad thing, because it causes you to "lose contact with the truth". To me, that sounds more like a leader that is afraid of losing his power because untethered empathy may cause the truth to come out and make them look bad.

Victims of sexual assault do not come forward just for fun. One needs only look at the cases of Christine Blasey Ford and Anita Hill to see the vitriol aimed at them. We unfortunately live in a society that lacks the compassion to believe a victim first and use it as a springboard to search for the truth. Instead, the victim is always asked questions such as, "What were you wearing?" or "Had you been drinking?" Within the Evangelical movement victims of infidelity or sexual assault have been told they haven't "been serving their husband's needs", which is revolting.

The author of Jesus & John Wayne, Kristen Kobes Du Mez, addressed this in an article for Baptist News:

> "The tendency to deny sexual abuse also exists at the pew level," she added. "You have good Christians in these communities come around and protect and defend the perpetrator for the sake of protecting his ministry and protecting the witness of the church. There are countless examples of this, and these are the patterns that we observe."[3]

3. Brumley, Jeff—Du Mez sees link between sexual abuse cover up and complementarian theology—*Baptist Global News*—https://baptistnews.com/article/du-mez-sees-link-between-sexual-abuse-cover-up-and-complementarian-theology/#.YWiFE9nMLop

Truth AND Consequences

That is both infuriating and heartbreaking. There is a lack of consequences because the truth is suppressed. That leads to a lack of compassion, and the church is called to act compassionately as one of its central tenets. Instead, there is fear from those in charge of losing the power (and sometimes great wealth) they have gained. Greed is a powerful temptation, especially when it comes with power over others. We unfortunately have too many that have given in to that greed, and it has resulted in them failing to exercise their responsibilities placed upon them in leadership. They are failing to serve the people they are supposed to serve, and instead they are preserving themselves first.

I feel for the members of the clergy that have bravely tried to stand their ground with the truth amid culture wars and toxic attitudes. Eric Atcheson, a minister in the Christian Church (Disciples of Christ) recently wrote a brilliant Twitter thread about his experience as a church minister and why he retired because of burnout:

> "Covid was a massive shock to the wider church—which was already frankly in a state of disrepair—but what covid really did was bring to the surface a *lot* of toxic-ish that was bubbling just underneath, which we clergy tried desperately to fix, or to at least keep at bay. That was a tough enough task pre-covid. Clergy are expected be prophetic but not in a way that offends anyone, to always be available but also find time to raise model families, and to lead but only from a position of servanthood. It's a fine—and often exhausting—line to walk."
>
> "Covid threw accelerant on all of that, like gasoline on a fire. Overnight, clergy had to also become professional IT techs as our churches—many of which had fiercely resisted technology to that point—were forced into the world of online worship, video streaming, and the like. Over the course of weeks, clergy had to become public health experts not only to safely lead our churches, but to act as a needed counterweight to the council chair or lead elder or board president whose brain got cooked on a diet of lies about ivermectin, masks, and vaccines."
>
> "Over the course of months, clergy had to become the mask police and social distancing enforcers. While we are often expected to be the morality police for a congregant's/congregation's pet issue, there was no way for us to enforce needed safety policies without outraging some."
>
> "I'll never forget what a trusted colleague said to me as we both wrestled with that reality: your people are going to be angry with you no matter what you do by now, at least let them be angry

Compassion

with you for saving their lives. And man, what a choice to have to consciously make."

"Meanwhile, as all this is happening, we had been trying to—and continued to—lead our congregations through extremely necessary reckonings around racial injustice, rights for LGBTQ persons, and anti-democracy authoritarianism that rose directly in response to those first two. As a young(ish) minister, I think of the future the (white) US church might've had if it weren't forcing its most diverse generation of clergy ever to choose between serving as the church's hospice chaplains and being run out of congregations for championing said diversity."

"Across all these fault lines + more, clergy became punching bags for other hurt or emotionally ill-equipped people. We became the targets of truly appalling behavior by those we were called to love, and especially by those whose behavior has long been enabled by their church. With each act of mistreatment, covenant between us and our churches was broken. With each insult at us, we fell further out of right relationship not only with the churches we serve, but with our vocation of ministry itself. The trust that made the vocation possible was gone. Without that trust, the ministerial vocation is finally no longer worth it. The very real joys of church ministry are no longer worth the deep woes. Why stay in low-paying jobs requiring odd hours, uncommon levels of stress, and increasingly frequent acts of deep disrespect?"

"We're not scrubs or rubes; in the mainline church we're expected to be well-trained, credentialed, and experienced. Yet we're treated like hired help, spiritual chamberlains for people who consume increasingly vast amounts of disinformation and resent having that challenged. I've said it before, but it bears repeating: we get our congregants for one day a week, maybe two. Fox News, OAN, Newsmax, etc. get them the other 5–6 days. And for claiming to be pro-church and pro-Christianity, those outlets are actively harming the fabric of the church."[4]

This is utterly heartbreaking to me. On his website Reverend Atcheson says he knew he was called to ministry as a teenager. As someone who has struggled greatly to find his calling, I am envious of this statement. He has since done his best to fulfill that calling and speak his truth, but he has been beaten down by those that do not trust or believe his expertise despite his

---

4. Eric Atcheson on Twitter, April 29, 2002—https://twitter.com/RevEricAtcheson/status/1520095327046545408?t=qIOOlep86NC1JP4voPkF7w&s=09

extensive training. He challenged his congregation to grow, and it seems as if he was broken personally for it.

We see this in other areas too, such as the exodus of teachers from that profession because of parental interference and culture war nonsense. If you are accosted in standing for truth, why wouldn't you get burnt out?

There is an industry in "the truth", and I fear it has led many astray. I use quotes around "the truth" because the industry in question tends to strain the definition of it. It is the industry that makes Facebook groups buzz and messages of "read this before Facebook gets rid of it" fly across screens. There is an allure to the nature of "learn about x thing that they won't tell you", or "THEY don't want you to hear Y thing." It's siren song invites us behind a curtain, where the "real truth" lies.

It is often more misinformation, and a consequence of it is the further factioning of our society and relationships. It is born out of the distrust of established systems and platforms for information. It comes from greed, too. There is a natural dislike of large news sources because they are more in it for the money and ratings (which they are), but the alternative becomes just another grift and distortion of the truth.

How do we discern what is truth? We saw during the COVID-19 pandemic that even professional credentials and years of clinical research didn't qualify as truth to some people. Too often the truth is dismissed because we don't want to hear it or, worse yet, we don't want to admit that a belief we had was wrong. The chapter on humility earlier in this book touched on the hesitance to admit wrong, but when we fail to do so, we often see more consequences at the expense of the truth.

Even worse, holding out against the truth even in the face of overwhelming evidence just amplifies the consequences. America has devolved into a society that fiercely holds its positions regardless of evidence of if we are right or wrong. I have joked that I am a white male in my 40s on the internet, so it is impossible for me to be wrong. Well, someone people really believe that. Political stances and outright, bold-faced lies that can easily be proven as lies that would have sunk political careers 15–20 years ago carry zero consequences because they can run successfully on a platform of "What are you going to do, vote for the other party?"

It comes back to humility and pride. Our pride is a difficult thing to overcome when it is related to truths that we don't want to hear. Some truths are going to hurt, but they need to be heard, whether we like it or not. The desire to be right is strong, even overwhelming. When it evolves

Compassion

into willful ignorance in the face of easily proven facts, it becomes a form of hubris that is damaging. It's how grifters take advantage of those desperate to hear they are in the right. It is how in the middle of a pandemic we have people trying to take horse de-wormer instead of following basic science. It is okay to trust God, but God also gives us plenty of gifts and knowledge to figure out His creation and improve our lives.

Cody Guitard describes this well in his blog on Ratio Christi:

> "We are told time and time again in Scripture that not everyone or everything that claims to be or even has the appearance of being of God is, in fact, of God (2 Cor. 11:13–15, 2 Tim. 3:5, Titus 1:16). The early church father Irenaeus rightly said: "Error never shows itself in its naked reality, in order not to be discovered. On the contrary, it dresses elegantly, so that the unwary may be led to believe that it is more truthful than truth itself." We are even warned in 2 Timothy 4:3–4 that "the time is coming when people will not endure sound teaching, but having itching ears they will accumulate for themselves teachers to suit their own passions, and will turn away from listening to the truth and wander off into myths.""[5]

That final verse from 2 Timothy is something that resonates in today's world, but it also raises the question of "Who is right, then?" Am I right because I am attempting to look at things from a Christ-centered view and what He did in the Gospels? Are the mentors I now view as having strayed from the very principles that they taught me right because they are older than me and confident in their faith? I really wish I had answers there, because if I had a definitive answer, it would make things a lot easier. Instead, I must go back to what I believe in and why I believe it, while attempting to be humble and admit to myself that maybe, just maybe, I am wrong.

It is something that causes my mind to churn way too much in those quiet moments. That question, "but what if I am wrong?" is loud when it is quiet. It is healthy to be that skeptical because it at least allows space for an open mind, but it still does not make one's faith any easier. There has been plenty of Scriptural evidence to support my point, but if you go looking, there is plenty of Scriptural evidence to support another point.

As Rachel Held Evans said earlier, the Bible is quite complex. I still think we all serve a large God that can handle all of us, different viewpoints and all.

5. Guitard, Cody, Discerning Truth in a World of Fake News and Fake Views—*Ratio Christi*—https://ratiochristi.org/blog/discerning-truth-in-a-world-of-fake-news-and-false-views/

Truth AND Consequences

Truth hurts. It hurts when we are confronted with our wrong-ness. It hurts when it is pointed out that we are not being compassionate. An obscure blog post from 2016 from a writer only identified as "Solomon" discusses the issue of truth and compassion very pointedly:

> "But I am of the mind that being nice is simply not enough. I am of the mind that following Christ in a way that is faithful cannot simply be conflated to "be nice". That being a good Christian is not rooted in simple asceticism or compliance. I am of the mind that our twisted sense of goodness is evil in better clothes. The Gospel of Jesus Christ calls us to the sanctification of liberation. And that liberation is not just for people who share our orientation, affiliation or station in life but to all of God's creation."[6]

I am a blunt person by nature, often to the point of not being nice. I suck at being courteous for the sake of being courteous and often see very little point in trying to dress something up as nice when it clearly is not. At work if I think a certain software we use or a service we use sucks, I am blunt in saying it sucks, then I try to back it up by bringing receipts as to why. In a way, this entire book is blunt. There are a lot of people that need to hear some things in a blunt way because being nice has not worked. I am also aware this is a character fault and it doesn't always work.

Solomon here is right though. Being nice isn't enough. Being nice is easy. It comes with words and makes us feel good. Actually *doing* something is much more difficult. This applies in many areas of life. It is great to talk about wanting to lose weight but doing something about it requires motivation and effort. Reaching out beyond our little social circles is similar. It means we must get outside of what makes us comfortable. It means we may have to associate with people that don't see things our way. It might even mean that our world view needs to be challenged.

But as I have said many times, challenging ourselves is a good thing. We learn by being challenged. I see it in my son. His is very stubborn, but I refuse to not challenge him because I know in the long run it is a good thing for him. It is a challenge for me too because the easy thing would be to sit back and do nothing, trusting others to challenge him. It is my job as a parent to challenge him.

A Christ-centered worldview is absolutely challenging too. Christ did not say, "Just be nice to everyone and it will all work out." He got his hands

---

6. Solomon—That was not very nice—*This Might Hurt A Little* blog—http://thismighthurtalittle.blogspot.com/2016/05/that-was-not-very-nice.html

dirty. He went out and worked with the outcasts of society. He walked into the temple and cleared it out. He healed the sick, fed the hungry, and taught others. He urged his disciples to go out and do the same, and when they were sitting around moping about His death, He showed up to give them the metaphorical kick in the butt they needed to go and do His work, then He provided the Holy Spirit to provide further motivation. His ultimate example of "doing something" was to take the world's sins to the Cross with Him.

Christ lived His truth, and the consequences are that we need to live it as well because He gave us the example. That example was not to sit around and judge, thinking that we are better because we know some truth, but to instead get out in the world, get our hands dirty, and live our lives with what He did as an example instead of sitting around waiting for Him to return and take all the good people away because "we are not of this earth anyway."

We live on this earth, in this reality, whether we like it or not. You know what though? Jesus lived on this earth too, and He didn't wait for someone else to the work he was called to do all the way to the Cross. The absolute least we can do is to follow His example.

8

"I Don't Know" is Okay

Having a great big Sam's Club-sized God is a wonderful thing, because that fact covers up a lot of deficiencies in faith. A big God can stand in when we are weak, and especially when we admit that we just don't know about something. It is hubris to think that we always have all the right answers. In truth, no one does, and if someone claims they have all the right answers they are lying.

Admitting we don't know something is deeply related to humility. It takes more courage to admit that we don't know something than it does to project false bravado and say we know it all. I think this is especially true as a parent. We want to project to kids that we are superheroes that stand in front of everything to protect them. In reality, I think it is better to have a healthy amount of humility and just say, "I don't know" sometimes. I may say it in exasperation to my son when he is asking his 29th question of the last 15 minutes, but I am also not afraid to say it concerning larger issues because it shows that even I am willing to set aside my pride and admit that I don't know it all, but I am willing to help find out together with him.

The inability to say "I don't know" is a strong contributor to a lot of problems we see in society today. Not only do people always want a definitive answer, but there are also numerous sources available that give said answers, even if they are wrong. In addition to that, you have the art of the grift. There are more than enough bad faith actors that are willing to take

Compassion

advantage of people's desire for answers for their own monetary gain. They will claim to know it all and be happy to tell you, all for a price.

This is not another takedown of one side or the other. Both try to sell easy answers. The easiest way to tell if it is a grift is if they are selling anything, pretty much. As someone who has worked for a long time in digital media, I know ad sales drive everything. My website and the podcasts I participate in all have ads but having ads on a college sports website or a silly sports podcast are far from dangerous.

When someone is selling answers to the tough questions or saying what people want to hear to backup already flawed beliefs it is awfully convenient that you can then "support their content," by "visiting this website and buying with offer code GIVEMEMYMONEY." This is not limited to conservative con men like Alex Jones, Ben Shapiro, and others. A comedy/history podcast I listen to called The Dollop does the exact same thing and given the commentary they have in every episode's story their leanings lie on the other end of the political spectrum.

And yes, I say this as you are holding a book in your hands or you're reading a file on a tablet that you likely paid for. I hope that you see from this chapter that I am up front in saying "I don't know" about myself, and I am even willing to admit that I might be wrong. Of course, if you have made it this far, that probably isn't a huge issue, so thanks!

There is no shame in, "I don't know". There is no shame in figuring things out away from those offering the easy answers. One of my latest struggles comes from the "I don't know" regarding compassion. As I mentioned earlier, we have people literally taking a de-wormer for horses to fight a virus instead of trusting well researched and proven science, all to make a point because someone with those easy answers decided they needed to push it as an agenda, and it was conveniently against the side they are carefully cultivated to disagree with in all things. It is absurd, yet some people truly believe in it. We are all taken advantage of for the profit of those more than happy to say whatever it takes to enrich their pockets.

How strong is this belief? You have people following to the point of dying, and that is what can make compassion so difficult. When COVID-deniers, anti-vaxxers, and their ilk end up dying because of their misguided beliefs the temptation is strong to spike the football with a well tweeted "They got what they deserved." Where is the compassion in that?

That is what causes me a deep ache. We are called to be compassionate beings, but the internal war of an "I don't know" on how to have that

"I Don't Know" is Okay

compassion vs. the desire to mock those who receive a dose of reality is strong. I must have compassion for the family members left behind to deal with these mistakes. I must have compassion for those still in the thrall of what I see as willful ignorance. I must have compassion and grace for those in my own circles that look the other way or try to explain away obvious truths because they are stuck in their own worldview and refuse to accept anything outside of it. I even must have compassion for those that died mostly because I don't understand why they felt that way, all to make a point that seems so misguided.

But I still admit that I just. Don't. Know. It is a deep struggle for me personally to find that compassion for those that have not only wronged, for those that I see as misguided, and for those that continue to do so despite any case I make against them. In a way, I envy their own faith and convictions, but it is very difficult to do the right thing and have compassion when I believe they are deeply in the wrong, especially when I still have that small voice in my head that says, "what if you're the one who is wrong?" That voice is small, but powerful, but I am willing to admit that it might be right.

It's okay to have that voice.

The world is a grim place and seems to be getting worse. I know the default answer of many in my life would be "well, we just need to reconcile ourselves with the world and Biblical principles." Unfortunately, it has been that way for centuries. America was founded as a "Christian nation" while its founders were perfectly okay with owning human beings. If you don't think racism is endemic in this country, then why was the original Constitution cool with counting slaves as $3/5^{ths}$ of a person?

It is not like world history is rife with peaceful utopias beforehand, either. War, injustice, bigotry, oppression, slavery, and other awful things have pretty much been around for all human history. At this point it is pretty much embedded in the nature of man. We even saw it in the Bible. The ancient Israelites, who have been the shining example of perfection in the eyes of many, committed plenty of atrocities.

I once heard that the only perfect person that ever lived was nailed to the Cross, and if that doesn't say something about the nature of man, I don't know what else does. Even though it is hard admit that imperfection in ourselves, to say that "I don't know", and admit it to others, it can be a strength.

Liza Babcock expressed this well when she wrote about the strength of saying "I don't know":

> "To state it plainly, humility keeps us honest. No one can say they have the complete picture, ever. At best, we can aspire to have a better partial picture than others with similar education/training. We've all succumbed at some point to the human inclination to fake it when we don't know the answer, or slant things our way to save face. But staying humble is good human capital. Strong people can afford to be humble while still pushing for better results. It's inspiring to see anyone—but especially our leaders—say "I don't know" when they really don't. We want our leaders to lead, and we want them to be human."[1]

Again, it comes back to having humility. It is a lost art. The world is calling for easy answers and a way to avoid that admission of "I don't know", but it becomes a fool's errand. There is folly in seeking that comfort of confirming your biases instead of just saying, "Hey, I don't know this, but that's okay." It leads to the dismissal of people that might know what they are talking about. Look at what 2 Peter 1:5–9 says:

> "**5** For this very reason, make every effort to add to your faith goodness; and to goodness, knowledge; **6** and to knowledge, self-control; and to self-control, perseverance; and to perseverance, godliness; **7** and to godliness, mutual affection; and to mutual affection, love. **8** For if you possess these qualities in increasing measure, they will keep you from being ineffective and unproductive in your knowledge of our Lord Jesus Christ. **9** But whoever does not have them is nearsighted and blind, forgetting that they have been cleansed from their past sins."

Our hubris is nearsighted. An unwillingness to shut up, admit we don't know something, and listen, makes us nearsighted. Theologian Thomas Merton said: "Pride makes us artificial and humility makes us real". The first warning bell that someone does not know everything or that they are lying is when they say that they know everything or have something all figured out. If someone is not strong enough to admit that maybe they don't know a specific answer it is usually a sign that they are trying to pull one over on people for their own benefit. At that point it is best to ignore them and try to figure things out for yourself, especially when they claim to have the inside track or secret knowledge that, "the experts don't want you to hear about."

---

1. Babcock, Liza—The Strength of 'I Don't Know'—*Ideas to Go*—https://www.ideas-togo.com/articles-on-innovation/the-strength-of-i-dont-know

"I Don't Know" is Okay

Remember: The world is waiting to tell you what to believe in and why to believe it if you're not secure in your own beliefs, and there are plenty of people out there willing to tell you if you use code GIVEMEMYMONEY for a special discount.

God gives us many gifts. They are blessings that strengthen and encourage us, but they are also ways that we can be a blessing to others. Many of these are outlined in 1 Corinthians 12:7–11:

> "Now to each one the manifestation of the Spirit is given for the common good. [8] To one there is given through the Spirit a message of wisdom, to another a message of knowledge by means of the same Spirit, [9] to another faith by the same Spirit, to another gifts of healing by that one Spirit, [10] to another miraculous powers, to another prophecy, to another distinguishing between spirits, to another speaking in different kinds of tongues, and to still another the interpretation of tongues. [11] All these are the work of one and the same Spirit, and he distributes them to each one, just as he determines."

Later, the chapter goes on to describe in metaphor how these gifts within the church (of which all human beings are a part of, whether they participate or not) work in conjunction with each other like the part of the human body:

> "[5] Now if the foot should say, "Because I am not a hand, I do not belong to the body," it would not for that reason stop being part of the body. [16] And if the ear should say, "Because I am not an eye, I do not belong to the body," it would not for that reason stop being part of the body. [17] If the whole body were an eye, where would the sense of hearing be? If the whole body were an ear, where would the sense of smell be? [18] But in fact God has placed the parts in the body, every one of them, just as he wanted them to be. [19] If they were all one part, where would the body be? [20] As it is, there are many parts, but one body."

This flies in the face of those that say they have all the answers and who refuse to admit they may not know something. We all have different parts to play. We are all called to different things. A football team made up of all kickers would not be very successful. You would never ask a kicker to play quarterback. It is not his specialty. Why, then, do we have people who have never worked in a specific field that takes years of training spouting opinions as if they held a PhD in said field? Worse, people believe them over the experts!

Compassion

You can say, "I believe in God and I don't trust science," but when you look at this part of 1 Corinthians it is not hard to see where God explicitly gives the gift of science and innovation to some of us so we can care for His creation. That's what a big God does! There is absolutely no shame in saying, "Well, I don't understand this, but maybe that other person does."

When I used to make TV commercials, I once had to make one for a small-town health clinic. Throughout the shoot one of the doctors at the clinic was micromanaging every aspect of the production. It got so bad I wanted to go to him and say, "Look, would you come to me if you broke your leg? No, because I am not a doctor. I don't have that knowledge. Now how about you let me use what knowledge I do have and make this commercial." The people who claim to know better than the experts in some other field are like that doctor trying to tell me how to make a TV commercial.

There is ample evidence throughout Scripture that God is fine with us receiving knowledge from others, and others can receive knowledge from us, because we live in society under his Dominion. Thankfully, in that Dominion, saying that you don't know something is perfectly okay.

9

At Your Service

IN ADDITION TO MY Christian upbringing, Scouting was a large part of my youth. I got involved in the Scouting movement as a Cub Scout in the first grade at age 7. From there, I like to say that I "turned pro" in Scouting. I worked all the way through Cub Scouts and Boy Scouts, becoming an Eagle Scout in 1997. I got to experience quite a bit in my time as a Scout, with trips all over the country, lots of nights camping, and two National Scout Jamborees. I even got to (very briefly) meet President Clinton (who at the time I was led to believe was pretty much Satan incarnate) at the second one in the summer of 1997.

Yes, that's me: Sports blogger, dad joke master, and meeter of Presidents.

The biggest thing that Scouting taught me was that service is critically important. Let's look at the 12 points of the Scout law:

A Scout is . . .

- Trustworthy
- Loyal
- Helpful
- Friendly
- Courteous

Compassion

- Kind
- Obedient
- Cheerful
- Thrifty
- Brave
- Clean
- Reverent

All of those are parts of compassionate living, and they lead to a life of service to others. One of the largest requirements of each rank in Scouting is time spent working on service projects. This culminates with the Eagle Scout project, which is a final exam of sorts. Instead of working in service of others in community service the Eagle Scout project is planned and organized by a Scout as the final test before becoming an Eagle. It is quite common for younger scouts to work their service time while working on someone else's service project, meaning that the benefit is twofold: The prospective Eagle Scout learns leadership skills in planning the project and carrying it out, while the next group of Scouts learns about service and how to eventually pull off their own projects once they advance high enough.

I have lost count of the number of Eagle Scout projects I worked on. There were at least a dozen in my time as I was going through those early years of Scouting. It meant a lot of painting, hauling junk, carpentry work, and more. These were all acts of compassion though, as we worked together as a team to accomplish a larger goal for our community.

The Bible has a lot to say about service, which is not a surprise, since Jesus was all about service. Jesus never put Himself above others, as it says in the Gospel of Mark: "And he sat down and called the twelve. And he said to them, "If anyone would be first, he must be last of all and servant of all."—Mark 9:35

Jesus' example is always an extremely humbling one. Even on the eve of His own death, he served his disciples by washing their feet. It is such an act of compassion that gets lost on the world. The idea of washing someone's feet today is not exactly appealing, but in the first century, it was even worse. We walk around in modern day shoes that protect our feet and keep them relatively clean, even if they are sweaty. In first century Palestine, however, it was a lot worse. People mostly wore sandals, so they walked around dusty roads that also contained animal manure and more.

At Your Service

It was not a job that anyone wanted, but the Son of God not only volunteered to do it, but he also did it with zeal. It was critically important to Him that one of the final lessons He shared with his disciples was one of submission and servitude, as outlined in John 13:12–17:

> "**12** When he had finished washing their feet, he put on his clothes and returned to his place. "Do you understand what I have done for you?" he asked them. **13** "You call me 'Teacher' and 'Lord,' and rightly so, for that is what I am. **14** Now that I, your Lord and Teacher, have washed your feet, you also should wash one another's feet. **15** I have set you an example that you should do as I have done for you. **16** Very truly I tell you, no servant is greater than his master, nor is a messenger greater than the one who sent him. **17** Now that you know these things, you will be blessed if you do them."

I cannot imagine a life without service to others. In a way, I feel like this entire book is an attempt to fulfill that, because if I can pass on even a small amount of what I have learned and have it make a difference in the world, it is worth it. It is what is asked of us, plain and simple.

The good news is that there are plenty of opportunities in which to serve, and all of them can be deeply fulfilling.

In the movie *Spaceballs* by Mel Brooks there is a great moment where the three main bad guys are on the bridge of their ship as everything in their plan begins to go haywire. Confused, President Skroob turns to Dark Helmet and just yells, "Do something!" In turn, Dark Helmet turns to Colonel Sandurz, the commander of the ship, and yells, "Do something!" The joke is completed when Colonel Sandurz, the guy with command of the ship they are on, picks up the intercom and yells, "Do something!"

Isn't that what life feels like sometimes? We get overwhelmed by a situation in front of us and all we feel like we can do is shout, "Do something!" up the line until we find someone that can do something about the problem. It becomes extra disappointing when nothing gets done. Society at large has a very big "Do something!" problem. We need to do something about climate change, but no one with any real power will do it. We needed to do something about COVID, but it was politicized for ridiculous reasons and only got worse as time went along, leading to misinformation and further polarization. We need to do something about injustice in the world, but those in power lack the willpower to come together and do anything about it.

Compassion

There are lots of reasons for this, and I know I have mentioned them in previous chapters. Greed is a large reason. Politicians on both sides are deeply financially invested in keeping things as they are without swinging one dramatic way or the other. Fear is another. We get paralyzed in the face of great change and miss opportunities. I know I have done it many times on a much smaller scale and missed out on a lot. For those much higher in the food chain, fear of losing power is a strong motivator. The fear of losing their power by being pushed out of office or the fear of being replaced by the crazier elements of their party is a big reason why few Republicans have stood up to Donald Trump. Conversely, the fear of losing office to more radical elements on either side has kept many Democrats straddling the middle instead of doing what is right.

Whether it is fear of losing power, fear of the unknown, greed, arrogance, or any other reason, the need to "Do something" about large important issues have pushed us to a point where compassion is often the first thing thrown out the window. Now we're in 2022, where there is very little compassion. There is only a tense stalemate with seething anger on both sides that robs compassion. Even worse, compassion is then seen as a weakness. The right views it as something to be taken advantage of. The left sees it as something undeserved when there is a comeuppance on the other side.

So how do we fix it? I really wish I had a more concrete answer, but I think it once again goes back to the small things. We can be better as a society, and it must start with our individual relationships. I know it is difficult to turn the other cheek when we are surrounded with people that are more than happy to slap that one once it is turned. I fear we may have moved past a point where trust can be restored, but somehow, we need to find a way to do better.

We are still asked to serve. We are still asked to provide support, help, and even encouragement for our friends *as well as* our enemies. If Christ can do this to the point of death, then we have to find a way to do it in the personal relationships we have. It begins in individual choices. I cannot fathom being a healthcare worker that still has the care and compassion to treat the very people that denied the existence of COVID. Those are people that rise above and need to be emulated. For every bloody riot, every war, every attack there are dozens of people that jump into the fray to aid those hurt on either side.

Faith is also important. Remember: We have a big, Sam's Club-sized God that can accomplish a whole lot more than we can ever hope to accomplish. He is a lot stronger than us and knows a lot more about the intricacies of the entire world. He's God. I am not. I can't even begin to understand even the smallest part of creation. Shoot, I can't even find something in my house half the time. Yes, it is trite and even somewhat hollow to just say, "have faith," but it does not make it any less true.

We are all given chances to "Do Something", be it large or small. The question is, are we ready to do it? It feels like the largest impediment to doing something is ourselves. One of my largest struggles is related to this. I become overwhelmed with life and either get paralyzed with so many things to do, or I "go kinetic", which means I exhaust myself with hours of trying to do too many things at one time. That, in turn, makes it difficult for me to enjoy free time because I cannot rest. I feel like I need to be doing something, and the cycle repeats itself.

That tells me that the "Do Something" sometimes means do nothing at all, or at the very least unplug. Rest is a huge part of life. It was designed to be part of life all the way back in Genesis when God Himself rested on the seventh day. While I don't believe so much in a literal seven-day creation (If that's how God did it though, who am I to argue), The idea of rest to calm ourselves is a wonderful one.

Jesus promises rest if we come to Him in Matthew. The Psalms constantly reference rest as a theme. In the book of Revelation, the Christian martyrs are promised rest beneath the very throne of God. If we do not take the time to truly rest and recharge, it makes the time where we do try to do something worse. Rest allows us to focus. It allows us to reinvigorate our energies instead of trying to push through with caffeine and the sheer force of will.

Rest is not part of American culture though. I love a meme that makes a regular appearance in a college football community I am a part of. It comes from Twitter user @samuel_pollen:

> "European out-of-offices: "I'm away camping for the summer. Email again in September"
>
> American out-of-offices: "I have left the office for two hours to undergo kidney surgery but you can reach me on my cell anytime""[1]

That is what it feels like a lot of the time. I am blessed with a day job that has a good life/work balance, but I have hobbies that I have also

---

1. Pollen, Samuel—https://twitter.com/samuel_pollen/status/1388121095597854725

Compassion

turned into jobs with my sportswriting. My day job has not always been as generous, either. There were days in my 20s where I would work all day on a Friday, then turn around and cover a high school basketball game, getting home after 10pm. When I was REALLY looking for permanent work, I would sometimes do this 2–3 times a week. It was draining in my 20s, and now that I am in my 40s it might kill me.

Our culture does not value rest, and that is why so many people feel uncomfortable when given the opportunity to do so. That desire to "Do Something" is overwhelming when we are bombarded from all sides with stimuli and crises, but it is okay if your "Do Something" is to take a rest. In fact, I encourage it.

Just tell me how to really do it once you figure it out.

10

I Can Do This All Day

THE MARVEL CINEMATIC UNIVERSE has made billions of dollars and has produced most of the highest grossing films of all time since debuting with *Iron Man* in May of 2008. One of the lead characters, of course, is Captain America, who was created in the 40s, frozen for over 70 years, and goes through a lengthy series of adventures. He is probably over 150 years old after time travel and such by the end of *Avengers: Endgame*. Since it is a series of comic book films, there is a lot of fighting. Cap gets into knockdown, drag out fights over the course of more than half a dozen films. In most of the films in the middle of a fight, often while losing, he picks himself up and has one of his signature lines:

"I can do this all day."

If any movie character knows perseverance, it is Captain America. He was picked on as a 90-pound asthmatic, experimented on, sent to fight the Nazis, frozen, fought interplanetary monsters, fought Hydra, fought the other Avengers, fought a genocidal Titan, time traveled, and more. Through it all, he perseveres. He remains the moral center of the Avengers, and never gives up trying to keep them on the right path.

My favorite verse in all the Bible is James 1:4—"Let perseverance finish its work so that you may be mature and complete, not lacking anything." While perseverance is important, I find the wording here from James to be interesting. The author is believed to be James, the brother of Jesus, who is very briefly discussed in the movie Dogma mentioned back in Chapter

6. We often think of perseverance as a characteristic we need to work on within ourselves, but James says that it must work in us.

We don't think of concepts such as perseverance, patience, compassion, empathy, or others as doing work in us. Throughout this work I have tried to stress the importance of being more compassionate, of being more empathetic, about working on ourselves like some sort of self-help mantra. I think our faith is a form of perseverance working in us. We trust that there is something more, and in return, that strengthens us.

There is a lot more to James when it comes to persevering. In chapter 2 he talks at length about faith without works:

> "**14** What good is it, my brothers and sisters, if someone claims to have faith but has no deeds? Can such faith save them? **15** Suppose a brother or a sister is without clothes and daily food. **16** If one of you says to them, "Go in peace; keep warm and well fed," but does nothing about their physical needs, what good is it? **17** In the same way, faith by itself, if it is not accompanied by action, is dead. **18** But someone will say, "You have faith; I have deeds." Show me your faith without deeds, and I will show you my faith by my deeds. **19** You believe that there is one God. Good! Even the demons believe that—and shudder."

This is central to the concept of perseverance. Some would argue that it says we can be saved by works, but I think it is the opposite. We are saved by grace through faith, but part of that transaction is that we then must do the work as a form of thanks for that freely given grace. It is action based on gratitude. In a way, we are called to "Do Something", which I talked about in the previous chapter. This is a clear call that once we have our faith, we are not to horde it. We are not to sit back and bask in it while casting aside others because of a difference belief. We are not to rest with an attitude of, "Well, I got mine and I am not of this world anymore, so I cannot be a part of it."

As the passage says, even demons believe in God, but they lack the works. This is a call to action, and it is where perseverance does work in us. We are called to move forward even when it is difficult. We are called to be compassionate and empathetic even when it runs counter to what we want to do. We do not have faith because of our works, but we complete the work we are called to do *because* of our faith.

We have to do this all day.

Sometimes perseverance is easy. We feel energized and it is easy to push through the challenges that seek to delay us. We wake up in the morning ready to tackle the day, the coffee is perfect, the emails are answered quickly and easily when we get to work, and it seems like nothing is a roadblock.

Other days are much harder. The coffee machine doesn't work at all. The emails are either too numerous or even worse, there are none when you really need a few in order to answer questions and complete your part of a job. The thick fog of fatigue takes over, and it is only 9:47am.

Perseverance is about more than just pushing through obstacles. Pushing through temporary obstacles is a short-term nuisance. Perseverance is breaking through repeated obstacles and refusing to quit, no matter how long it takes.

In writing this book I had to learn about perseverance. There were days where the words flowed like water, and I would have 1,500 of them in the rough draft down in less than an hour. There were other days, even as I was writing this very chapter, where I had a flashing cursor and nothing happening as I did not know where to go. It was hard to admit that sometimes I just needed to step away, especially if I had recently had one of those days there the words came easy. Eventually I even set the whole thing aside for a few months after the initial draft was done and I wasn't sure if would ever go further. I stuck with it through my own doubt though, and now it is in your hands.

What kept me going was that I knew I was supposed to do it. It is very hard to explain, but it just *felt* like something I was supposed to do, even if I didn't know where I was going with it as I was in the middle. It took a lot of prayer, but when I would doubt if I should keep going, I almost always felt a gentle "yes" even during one of those blocks. Perseverance is moving forward, no matter how slow that forward movement is. Sometimes the hardest thing to overcome is ourselves.

Even the God of the Bible had to learn this. Remember, the Bible was written by dozens of authors across hundreds of years all over the world from Rome to Babylon with each author having a different vision of who God was. The author of Genesis described a God that was not patient with mankind at all. Just look at the Flood. There are several other examples in the Old Testament of God being quite vengeful. The Bible shows that God (at least the version presented over the course of it) has persevered with mankind, all the way to the culmination of that persevering compassion with the death of His Son on the Cross for our atonement.

I know it is hard to think of God persevering with us, especially when so much of what we are called to do is to persevere with Him and move forward. Let's face it though, we haven't exactly been the greatest stewards of the Creation that He has given us, yet He still has not come down to hit the "smite" button and take us all out Old Testament-style (as much as there are those in society that would welcome that). Once again, I go back to Dogma when a very upset angel in Bartleby, played by Ben Affleck, shows how easily God could be frustrated with us:

> "The humans have besmirched everything bestowed on them. They were given Paradise, they threw it away. They were given this planet, they destroyed it. They were favored best among all His endeavors, and some of them don't even believe He exists. And in spite of it all, He's shown them infinite f***ing patience at every turn."[1]

How is the patience God has shown mankind, despite the terrible things we have done to His creation, not an example of His perseverance? How is it not an example of His compassion?

Christ is the ultimate example of perseverance, and the main sign that God Himself perseveres with us. Let's try to look at the life of Christ from a completely secular perspective. Even if you don't believe in God at all, you must admit that the influence of a man named Jesus has been remarkable in world history.

Jesus was born into the Roman Empire at a time called Pax Romana, which is Latin for "Roman peace". It was a roughly 200-year period generally regarded to have begun with the ascension of Caesar Augustus in 27 BC until the death of Marcus Aurelius in 180 AD.

During this period the Roman Empire reached its largest territorial extent. It ranged from southern Egypt in the south, to the modern-day Netherlands in the north, to modern day Spain in the west, and to Syria and Palestine in the east. At its height, there were more than 70 million people under the rule of Rome, which at the time was maybe a quarter of the world's total population.

This was a vast empire, one of the largest the world had seen to that point. Jesus was born into it during the reign of Caesar Augustus, who is mentioned as the reigning Emperor in the Christmas story presented by Luke. Judea was mostly a crossroads for the Roman Empire, serving as a land route between Egypt and Syria, two valuable Roman possessions. It wasn't much more than a roadway between two vitally important areas, much like how a smaller city like Lafayette, Indiana might be a regional

---

1. Smith, Kevin—*Dogma*—View Askew Productions—Lions Gate Films—1999

center for shopping, hotels, etc. along a highway between two major cities in Indianapolis and Chicago.

Palestine in the First Century was a footnote in this grand empire. There were no Roman legions. There were a few officials, but the area was ruled by Herod the Great under a system of "You keep the peace, and we make sure you stay in power" agreement with Rome. The Jewish areas of Palestine governed themselves on a local level and were generally left alone. Much of the area was "as long as you stay out of trouble, we'll leave you alone."

While Jesus was born in Bethlehem, His family was from Nazareth and that is where He grew up. It was not a prominent area. Even the Gospels viewed Nazareth as an unassuming place, as John 1:46 even says, "'Nazareth! Can anything good come from there?' Nathanael asked," when the first disciples are called. Nazareth was the backwater of a backwater in the largest empire on earth. If Jesus were to come about today in modern America, it would be like if He came out of the Idaho Panhandle: Yeah, it's part of America, but there is not much there of note.

Some scholars estimate that there were about 400 people in Nazareth at the time of Jesus' birth. His father was a carpenter. He would have learned the same skills as His father, and it is very likely He worked in obscurity for 30 years of His life. That's quite a while, especially when we live in an age where teenagers become world famous because of TikTok videos. Once again, this shows His humility. Here is a man that went about the world stating He was the very Son of God during His public ministry, but in His humility, He stayed at home for 30 years likely working as a mere carpenter.

So, consider this: Jesus was from nowhere. His background was from nothing. He was not a member of the Jewish religious elite. He was not a Roman citizen. He was a nobody from a forgotten corner of the realm that wasn't even held in high esteem in Jewish circles, all while the Jews were a religious minority among dozens of Gentile sects in this nearly forgotten province.

Even if you look at His life from a strictly secular perspective it is remarkable that this one person had such an effect on world history. The Bible targets His public ministry at around three years before he was crucified. The Gospels tell most of His story, but they are obviously slanted by those who wrote them. There are non-Christian sources such as Josephus and Tacitus that help establish that yes, Jesus was a real man that lived in First Century Palestine, so it is very likely He existed because those two

Compassion

authors wrote independently of each other. Josephus was a Jewish historian and Tacitus was a Roman historian.

New Testament scholar Ed Parish Sanders is one of the leading scholars in what can be called historical Jesus research. He has proposed the following "indisputable facts" about a historical Jesus[2]:

- Jesus was a Galilean preacher.
- His activities were confined to Galilee and Judea.
- He was baptized by John the Baptist.
- He called disciples.
- He had a controversy at the Temple.
- Jesus was crucified by the Romans near Jerusalem.
- After his death his disciples continued.
- Some of his disciples were persecuted.

We see from this that He came from nowhere, got 12 guys to follow Him around, He clashed with the religious elite of the day, He was crucified as an afterthought by Pontius Pilate (in the Gospels Pilate really does not want to get involved), and His disciples continued his message after He was crucified.

Even in looking at the disciples we see that they were unassuming. Peter, James, John, and Andrew were fishermen. Nathanael was a scholar. Matthew was a tax collector. Simon was a religious zealot who hated Rome. Little is known about some of them, but they were all like Jesus in that they were nobodies. If you were casting a movie where a group of people save the world you wouldn't start with these guys.

Can you see the perseverance of God here though? Jesus was one nobody. The Twelve were his first followers and worked diligently to spread the Message with many of them martyred for their work, but they were still 12 men that had no real outside authority. On the day of Pentecost, Acts says that three thousand were added to their number. That number further went out into the world along the roads and ships of the empire and spread the Gospel even further. While there would be persecution of Christians from Rome during the early church, there is little question historically that it grew like wildfire. Within a few decades Paul was preaching the Gospel

---

2. *Authenticating the Activities of Jesus* by Bruce Chilton and Craig A. Evans 2002

in Rome itself. Eventually, Constantine the Great would become the first Roman leader to convert to Christianity.

Even if God isn't real. Even if it is all a coincidence and Jesus was not the son of God, in the span of about 300 years a man whom no one had ever heard of before he was 30 years old was raised up as a deity by the largest empire in the world. Even when you take in the vastness of the Roman Empire and its network of established trade that allowed information to flow faster than ever before that is remarkable.

And today, that influence continues. Think about the term "First century" above. Clearly, there was history before that. We have a dividing line of "BC" and "AD" that was established based on the birth of Jesus. Yeah, He was a nobody from nowhere, but our modern-day calendar is centered on His birth. I do recognize there are Muslim, Jewish, Chinese, and other calendars out there, but the vast majority of the world runs on a calendar based on Jesus. What other person in human history can make that claim?

Also, for good or ill, much has been done in His name. Yes, this includes slavery, oppression, colonization, and a myriad of other awful things that should never be whitewashed from history, but there is art, music, charities, works, and more that had showed the best that humanity has to offer, all in the name of Jesus.

How is that not God's perseverance? Even if you do not believe in God, it is remarkable that the character of Jesus is even remembered by a single person almost 2,000 years later considering His background. His legend has endured through the centuries despite enormous odds given where the story began. It took decades for His story to reach Rome itself and even longer to spread further, but that story, even without the divine background behind it, is an incredible testament to perseverance.

By adding compassion and empathy to that perseverance we can accomplish so many things. We can do better.

11

All Things Being Equal

When I was in high school, I had a friend that told me a possibly apocryphal story about a geometry test. We were learning geometric proofs, which was something I struggled with before eventually understanding them. This friend of mine supposedly knew someone who, when presented with an exam equation of "Prove (random geometry term) is equal to (other random geometry term)," wrote as an answer, "Nah, I'll take your word for it."

To this day I don't remember the terms that were supposed to be part of the proof or the kid that supposedly wrote it, but "Nah, I'll take your word for it" is hilarious to me. On the surface, math seems so simple. You're trying to find balance and get one side of an equation to equal another. If you can do that, great! There are varying degrees of difficulty out there and I have forgotten basically all my high school Calculus (sorry, Mr. Kunkle), but many of the mysteries of our world have been solved by balancing those equations.

Unfortunately, equality in the real world has been a lot harder to find. We're taught that America is this great country where everyone has a fair shot, but this is also the same country that said people with a different skin color only counted as three fifths of a person when it was founded. The Declaration of Independence did say that all men were created equal, but a good portion of the Constitution clearly outlines that some are more equal than others.

In other places in the world things are far worse. This is why I am appreciative that Christ preached a true equality. There are dozens of examples throughout the Gospels and in the rest of the New Testament that Christ's message was not for the elite, but for everyone. We're all sinners, and unworthy, but Christ makes us worthy. That grace is equally distributed. You don't get to go in line ahead of others because you prayed harder, voted for a certain candidate, had more money, or for any other reason.

Where does equality truly begin? Not to sound trite (okay, it sounds trite), but the children are the future. All of today's adults were once kids, and they wouldn't have learned about discrimination if not for the adults teaching them. It is a trait that can be unlearned, but it is easier to not learn it in the first place.

My son is nine, and he is half Hispanic. I am proud of his heritage because he has something I will never have. From the family research I have done I don't have a single ancestor I have found that came to the United States after about 1850 or so. My wife's family came from Colombia in the late 1970s, however, and her parents eventually became naturalized citizens. For this being an "equal" society, I have seen first-hand the challenges they have faced being immigrants that do not speak English as their first language. It is one of those things that has influenced my views as an adult.

When he was in day care, we were incredibly blessed to have an older African American woman with a small, private day care take care of him. "Miss Pammommie", as she is called, welcomed us into her business with open arms and is one of the kindest and most devout women I have ever had the pleasure of knowing. She is the type of woman that studies her Bible daily. I have seen it in her office, and it is well loved, with dogeared pages and copious notes scribbled in the margins. It is her treasure. Her work is a true reflection of her values and her faith that she feels is her responsibility to pass on. This woman has been gifted with a caring spirit that shines each day, and she celebrates that many of her babies have grown into young men and women of character thanks to her guidance.

My son was in her care from the time he was two months old until he went to kindergarten, and it was an amazing and fulfilling experience for us. It also went beyond the early educational opportunities he received (such as sitting with older children even as an infant during story time and such). It was seeing true equality in action at a base level.

From day one the expectation was the that the children were to respect themselves and each other. This lesson was taught before many of the kids could talk and put into action as the children grew older. They learned with each other and helped each other. They saw each other as fellow kids,

Compassion

and their respective backgrounds were to be always respected. That was Miss Pammommie's way, and if you didn't go her way there would be age-appropriate consequences until you went her way. The expectations were clear and concise, much like the same expectations my dad laid out on the day I moved into my college dorm as a freshman.

The children in her care came from a variety of backgrounds. We were blessed enough to be able to simply write a check every week, on time, for her services. Other families in her care were not so blessed. Many were on government assistance. Regardless of background, Miss Pammommie made sure that children who came to her received the same opportunities. She would not turn a child away that needed care. Period. Even since my son "graduated" from her care I have stayed in touch with her and offered to help however I can because I value what she does so much.

My son also spent time with children of different races from day one. There were African American kids, white kids, Asian kids, etc., and they were all taught to respect each other first. Now that he is older, he is sadly starting to learn that people are not treated equally for their skin color or their background, or even that people would look down on him because of his background and ethnicity. To him, this type of discrimination is a foreign concept, and he simply doesn't understand why people would do it.

This is not a difficult concept to understand. If we teach kids from the beginning to treat people with equality and respect it will come. Respect is a large part of equality, and with equality comes compassion, which is the central theme of this work. Kindness, respect, and basic human decency should not be lost arts. They should be central lessons we teach our children as building blocks to empathy and compassion as adults.

They also must be examples of our own behavior. We can have outstanding adults care for kids like Miss Pammommie and her daughter, Miss Shawn, who have influenced hundreds of children over the years. If we do not back up their efforts as parents their work is in vain. It is not that hard to treat people like human beings instead of shunning them. It harkens back to that whole "judge not, lest ye be judged" thing.

One of the most misunderstood parts of Scripture is that of "Biblical Gender Roles". The basic idea is that the man is the head of the household and what he says goes. There are a lot of writers and theologians out there with some Very Strong Opinions (emphasis mine) that wives can make decisions and run the home, but ultimately, they cannot conflict with the "will of their husband".

As always, they back this up with cherry picked Scripture, especially 1 Corinthians 11. If you do a simple search on "Biblical Gender Roles" you get into some real wild stuff like, "If women have children later in life the world population will keep declining!" Nevermind that it has exploded exponentially in the last century and that the planet is catching fire because of it. There is also plenty of Biblical evidence that women are equal to men. Author Phillip B. Payne wrote about this in the Priscilla Papers, an academic journal of CBE International:

> "Is the Bible divided on the issue of gender? Many highly respected evangelical scholars believe there is a tension in the Bible between affirmations of gender equality and gender roles. Can we arrive at a consistent biblical position without doing violence to the text? Need one sacrifice good exegesis at the altar of systematic theology? Surely, good exegesis and good systematic theology go hand in hand. I have prayerfully wrestled for forty-one years with the texts' apparent contradictions on gender and can honestly say that the biblical texts themselves have transformed my understanding. From creation to new creation, the Bible's message about gender in the church and marriage consistently affirms the equal standing of man and woman."[1]

Even in the examples he cites there are contradictions. Men and women were created equal in Genesis 2, but in Genesis 3, as the result of the Fall, "He will rule over you" is stated about Adam over Eve. There are lots of references to women leading men in the Old Testament. In the New Testament Jesus also did not hold men over women according to Mr. Payne:

> "Jesus in all his words and deeds left us an example to treat women as equals with men, never subordinated or restricted in role (Matt 12:49–50; 15:38; 25:31–46; Mark 3:34–35; Luke 8:21; 11:27–28). His treatment of women as equals defied the judicial, social, and religious customs of his day. On judicial matters where women's rights were curtailed, such as regarding adultery and divorce, he treated men and women equally. In a society that regarded women as less intelligent and less moral than men, Jesus respected women's intelligence and spiritual capacity, as is evident in the great spiritual truths he originally taught to women such as the Samaritan woman (John 4:10–26) and Martha (John 11:25–26)."

1. Payne, Philip B.—The Bible Teaches the Equal Standing of Man and Woman—*Priscilla Papers, The Academic Journal of CBE International*—https://www.cbeinternational.org/resource/article/priscilla-papers-academic-journal/bible-teaches-equal-standing-man-and-woman

Compassion

Overall, Mr. Payne's piece is a great takedown from beginning to end in Scripture of examples where men and women have equality. If you have an agenda though, you can find supporting evidence for it in the Bible. This applies both ways. I cannot say, definitively, which way is right and which way is wrong. I tend to side with the view that women are equal partners with men, but I also recognize that my view is skewed by many factors, including being married to a woman who would do the exact opposite of any edict I handed down "because I was the man" just to spite me.

Saying that women are not equal to men reduces their role to automatons that are not allowed to think for themselves or make their own decisions, and those that practice "Biblical gender roles" believe that women should be happy for husbands to relieve them from that "burden" and let them control the home. This can lead to situations where domestic abuse can go unreported out of fear. If it is reported to church authorities too much of the blame is placed on the woman for "not respecting her role", and she can even be blamed for "not doing enough to meet her husband's needs". It is a sad situation, and another example where we see power corrupting.

Even further, the oft-cited reasoning behind "Biblical Gender Roles" comes from Ephesians 5, so let's take a closer look:

> "21 Submit to one another out of reverence for Christ."
> "22 Wives, submit yourselves to your own husbands as you do to the Lord. 23 For the husband is the head of the wife as Christ is the head of the church, his body, of which he is the Savior. 24 Now as the church submits to Christ, so also wives should submit to their husbands in everything."
> "25 Husbands, love your wives, just as Christ loved the church and gave himself up for her 26 to make her holy, cleansing her by the washing with water through the word, 27 and to present her to himself as a radiant church, without stain or wrinkle or any other blemish, but holy and blameless. 28 In this same way, husbands ought to love their wives as their own bodies. He who loves his wife loves himself. 29 After all, no one ever hated their own body, but they feed and care for their body, just as Christ does the church—30 for we are members of his body. 31 "For this reason a man will leave his father and mother and be united to his wife, and the two will become one flesh.""—Ephesians 5:21–31.

Before we even get into wives submitting to husbands, we see that we are submit to each other. That sounds an awful lot more like equality as opposed to a "weaker sex" being constrained to serve the "stronger sex".

All Things Being Equal

The next part does, indeed say that wives are to submit to their husbands, but as the church submits to Christ. Christ did not lead by a domineering personality, but by quiet submission and humble service. His humility, compassion, and supplication stand out, so men are called to lead out of humility and compassion.

Also, we further see that husbands are not getting off scot free here. They, too, are called to love, but as Christ loved the church and gave Himself up for it. Christ was submissive to the point of the Cross for the sake of the church, so husbands need to be ready to be submissive to their wives as well if wives are supposed to represent the church. It becomes a symbiotic relationship instead of a dominant/submissive one.

Finally, we see that "two will become one flesh. That implies a working relationship and a synchronicity. We know that the right brain works very differently from the left brain in terms of creativity, control of the body, etc. It still functions as one brain. Each half is separate, but equal because one cannot work without the other. We see a similar example here in Ephesians 5. Yes, men and women are different. They have different strengths and weaknesses, but they cannot function in a marriage if one is fully submissive to the other. That creates a dangerous imbalance, and I think Ephesians 5 here shows that one side is not to dominate the other, but to complement the other.

As always, we need to use discernment. It is very likely that the people preaching Biblical Gender Roles would have never gotten this far in this book. In fact, if they made it past the introduction, I would be shocked. There is more than enough Scriptural evidence that speaks to the equality of women, so I will go ahead and side with that. If I am wrong, that judgment is only up to God.

If women are not in equal standing to men, cannot make their own decisions at home, and should not be in positions of power over men, why didn't Jesus say anything about this? Here is what Violet McDaniel had to say about a woman's place in first century Palestine:

> "Women were to be unobserved in public. The veil was one symbol that reflected this status in society. The veil was a requirement for every married woman. In addition to being a symbol of modesty and virtue, the veil also indicated a woman's married status and subordination to her husband. In keeping with the idea that women were to be unobserved in public, men were not supposed to look at married women, converse with women in public, or even give a woman a greeting when they passed on the street. The

Compassion

oral law stated, "Let no one talk with a woman in the street, no, not with his own wife." It was unusual for a Jewish teacher to converse with a woman in a public place. The rabbis taught that women were not to be saluted or spoken to in the streets, and not to be instructed in the law. Jewish women were not as restricted in public appearance as Greek women, but did not have the freedom of first century Roman women."[2]

That sounds an awful lot like the dream of many of these "Biblical Gender Roles" people, yet it was very clearly NOT the practice that Jesus Himself had with women. In John 4: 1–26 we have a very detailed account of Jesus speaking with a Samaritan woman at a well. Before you even get into the different gender roles in fist century Palestine, the Samaritans and the Jews hated each other for multiple centuries dating back to the Old Testament book of Nehemiah. Their religion was considered heresy, and upstanding Jews didn't associate with them, let alone speak to them.

This is the first thing the Samaritan woman mentions when Jesus asks her for a drink. Still, Jesus spoke to her. In fact, He did more than speak to her. He explained much of her life story and explains that He was the Messiah offering reconciliation. He was a Jewish man, speaking to a woman who was not His wife, and she was a member of a hated enemy. This is the type of thing that drove the Pharisees crazy.

After their discussion the disciples come back, and they are dismayed that Jesus would even speak to her. She goes and alerts the people in the nearby town about Jesus, and eventually many Samaritans believe in Jesus because of her testimony. A simple conversation became a chance to spread His ministry.

By the standards at the time, Jesus had no reason whatsoever to even acknowledge this woman's existence, let alone treat her with kindness, compassion, and empathy. Since she was an unmarried woman living with another man, she was not high in the social hierarchy, yet Jesus accomplished great things by just speaking to her, then trusting *her* to act as a leader of her people to Him.

We see other examples in the Gospels and beyond of women serving in vital roles in the early church. Mary Magdalene is not only the first person to witness the empty tomb and meet a resurrected Jesus, she is also the one that goes back to the rest of the disciples and wakes them up by

---

2. McDaniel, Violet—A Woman's Place in the First Century—*Truth Magazine*— http://www.truthmagazine.com/archives/volume44/V4405040008.htm

saying, "quit your moping, Jesus is alive!" Mary, the mother of Jesus is held in extremely high regard today throughout the church. Priscilla, wife of Aquila, had an extremely prominent role as a leader of the early church.

This is not the only example of Jesus preaching equality, either. We are commanded to "love our neighbors as ourselves" in Mark 12. In Luke 14 the "the poor, the crippled, the lame, and the blind" are to be invited to feasts. Even on the Cross it is not beneath Him to offer salvation to the condemned thief dying next to him.

There are hundreds of examples of calls for equality in other parts of the Bible too. Even Leviticus, the same book often cited when people are looking for a good zinger to back up their biases, has:

> "When a stranger sojourns with you in your land, you shall not do him wrong. You shall treat the stranger who sojourns with you as the native among you, and you shall love him as yourself, for you were strangers in the land of Egypt: I am the Lord your God."—Leviticus 19:33–34.

We lose nothing by treating people with equality and basic human kindness. The Bible is extremely clear that we are called to do it. That's why I don't understand why it is such a difficult concept for much of the modern American church to understand. I see too much of the Evangelical movement invested in ways to hold on to political and earthly power that they have far strayed from much of the true message of what Christ (and others!) in the Bible taught. Instead, we see a concession of their values in the pursuit of power. Even worse, they use the Cross to justify their actions.

Jesus stood up for the marginalized and the forgotten against the elite of His day. He very clearly spells out that we are to take care of these people. Rather than answer this call, we see "culture wars" of people pushing back against the marginalized that are trying to stand up for themselves. A rainbow flag suddenly becomes "the gay agenda forcing its views on me," or a simple greeting of "Happy holidays" to acknowledge that yes, several religions around the world happen to all have their holidays at the same time of year is, "A war on Christmas". When you have news programs and pundits losing their minds because a Starbucks Cup is plain red and does not have an ornate depiction of the Baby Jesus in the manger, we have clearly lost the narrative here. At that point it is no longer about the Gospel. It is about forcing your ideas and biases onto others, and the Gospel of berating, as I see it, is not one that bears fruit.

Compassion

It is absurd. You have people that have never been persecuted for a single second of their lives crying persecution because those that have faced actual trials and true inequality have the audacity to stand up and say, "no more." That is not what the Bible has in mind at all. It is not some ideal kumbaya where everyone holds hands and dances in a circle, but we can do better. We are called to do better. By starting at an individual level, with compassion and humility, we can be better.

12

This is Only a Test

THE SIMPSONS IS A show that proves God loves us and wants us to be happy. I haven't watched many of the newer episodes for years now, but seasons 2 through about 10 are timeless classics that only get better with age. In season 6 Homer loses a bunch of money investing in pumpkins and must go to Marge's sisters, Patty and Selma, for a loan to pay for his mortgage. It is a rough time for Homer, and he wonders aloud to Marge if God is trying to tell him something:

> Homer:
> "God is teasing me. Just like he teased Moses in the desert."
>
> Marge:
> "*Tested,* Homer. God *tested* Moses."[1]

There is no question that God tests us. Yes, when we are being tested it can feel like we are being teased. Even Jesus was tested with His 40 days in the wilderness. He made it through but being the Son of God helped. His trial in the wilderness was more of a test against temptation, but there are a variety of tests in life. Our patience is tested. Our values are tested. Even our very faith is tested.

As you read this, I hope we are finally on the permanent downside of the COVID-19 Pandemic. We have dealt with this pandemic for two years

1. Homer vs. Patty and Selma—*The Simpsons*—Season 6, Episode 17

Compassion

at this point, and it is a test. Clearly, it has influenced the previous chapters of this book. Living with it every day for two years has been exhausting.

There was the uncertainty of the first few weeks. Then, there was the boredom as quarantine dragged on. Next there was impatience as it was clear it would be around for a while a potential vaccine, seen in the summer of 2020 as the endgame, was developed and tested. There was the waning of restrictions, often out of impatience, as the pandemic became even more politicized. The brutal wave of winter gave birth to a spring where the vaccine was finally ready and numbers dropped, only for the Delta variant to come roaring back in August just as we had found our way out. The same vaccine that was touted as being developed by great leader Trump was suddenly an evil tool of tyranny because the person pushing it was not Trump (indeed, even he was booed when he pushed it at a rally in Alabama). In December 2021 and January 2022, you had the Omicron variant that caused cases to skyrocket to over 1 million per day in the U.S. alone at its height. What was "going to go away in a few weeks" was at its worst almost two years deep.

And this was only our experience in the United States. Other countries had it better. Poorer countries had it far worse. Here in the United States, we also had the pleasure of it happening in the middle of an election year, so it was fully politicized for maximum gain on both sides, thus making matters even worse in the long run because we currently live in a world where if one side says something, the other side sees it immediately as 100% wrong despite any evidence otherwise. Instead of banding together to do the right thing the bickering and squabbling began almost immediately.

It has been exhausting, and it continues to go on. It feels like an endurance trial, and compassion and empathy are at an end. Even though I fully disagree with anti-vaxxers and COVID-deniers, I find myself deeply troubled when people try to spike the football on those that catch this terrible disease because of their denial. I am way too active on Twitter for my own good, so I see all the "ha ha, sucks to be you" tweets when some conservative radio host or anti-vax grifter comes down with it and admits they are sick. I even want to join in because I am so tired of dealing with all of it. It is natural to want to say, "Good, now maybe they can have their nose rubbed in their wrongness."

That is not what I am called to do though. It is one of many tests I face. I must humble myself and still show empathy even when, if the tables were turned, the same people would not show me empathy. Paul spoke of this in Ephesians 4:31–32:

> "**31** Get rid of all bitterness, rage and anger, brawling and slander, along with every form of malice. **32** Be kind and compassionate to one another, forgiving each other, just as in Christ God forgave you."

We have to do better. We must *be* better, even if it goes against every other instinct. We are directly called to be kind and compassionate to one another. I know it is hard because I live in the real world. It is not what humans do well, whether you are a devout member of the church every Sunday or someone who has never set foot in one. Compassion takes action. It takes intent.

Testing our faith is good. Mine is one that has constantly been questioned. Growing up I was always told that "we are not of this world," but I was the outsider in my church youth group. I went to secular concerts. I would miss youth group because of other school activities. I even went to a large state school instead of the small Wesleyan university, to much scandal! Seriously, I had people tell me they would pray for me because I was going away to a non-Christian school. I was viewed with a wary eye because "I went to the city school" (my high school had about 2,000 students) instead of the school of about 300 that most of the kids in my church went to.

I always had my faith, but it never felt strong enough. I saw others are being much more faithful and devout for reasons I couldn't understand. I felt like I wasn't praying hard enough or that I was missing something when I would read the Bible. I questioned why it didn't speak to me in the same ways it spoke to others. Now I know that this comes from having a different experience than others.

As I grew older, I started to see life differently. That view of "we are not of this world" seemed almost fatalistic, like we're supposed to be waiting around to be removed from it. In reality, we do live in this world. Yes, it is a fallen and broken one with lots of injustice, but we are called to live in it and be compassionate, not wall ourselves off with others that only reinforce how right we think we are. We're called to make it better.

In the past year I have had my faith tested even more. As I mentioned in the first chapter, I have struggled mightily with those that taught me many of the values I hold dear. I see their actions in the present day and compare them with the actions that I saw from them while I was growing up and I see hypocrisy. As a result, I have questioned if my faith was as strong as I thought. I have questioned that I might be in the wrong in this

Compassion

case despite the values I was taught leading me otherwise. I have questioned if these mentors were wrong all long and even if God Himself doesn't exist. The good news is that we're both wrong because no one has truly figured it out yet, and no one ever will because we're not meant to. That has given me an unusual amount of peace.

These seasons of testing are not fun, but they are critical learning experiences. I will admit that I still don't know what I am learning from this time of testing or when it will end. Some days, it seems to get worse. It is hard to know the answers when even the questions seem unclear. The important part is to be open and willing to learn. A lot of personal growth comes from simply being tested. We have to be willing to accept these tests and learn from them, whatever those lessons may be.

I will be the first to admit that I don't know everything. I don't even want to be considered an expert on pretty much anything in this book. It is written mostly out of a test of my own faith in an attempt to get people to examine themselves and seek answers on their own. Too many in society claim to have exclusive knowledge that sets them apart. I once again must look at the book of James and what it says in Chapter 2, verses 13–17:

> "13 Who is wise and understanding among you? By his good conduct let him show his works in the meekness of wisdom. 14 But if you have bitter jealousy and selfish ambition in your hearts, do not boast and be false to the truth. 15 This is not the wisdom that comes down from above, but is earthly, unspiritual, demonic. 16 For where jealousy and selfish ambition exist, there will be disorder and every vile practice. 17 But the wisdom from above is first pure, then peaceable, gentle, open to reason, full of mercy and good fruits, impartial and sincere."

There is an entire industry that is not meek in its wisdom. There are dozens of podcasts, radio shows, news networks, and everything that thrive on selfish ambition. In fact, I view pretty much any cable news, pundit radio shows, or pundit podcasts as absolute flaming garbage because they are all based on selfish ambition. They thrive on creating division and turning away from compassion and empathy. If you look closely too, they are driven more by profit than anything, because those behind them conveniently get a lot of money to spew their views.

In a way, these are all tests. Do we want the easy answers they peddle that are already in line with our preconceived beliefs, so they are what we want to hear, or do we want to be tested and see if maybe, just maybe we are wrong? Being tested is good. It opens the door to compassion and empathy because we start to see those others outside of our little circles are people in need of empathy and compassion.

There is not a doubt in my mind that this country is currently being tested in terms of feeling compassion for others. I also do not have any doubt that it is failing said test, quite spectacularly. You have an Evangelical movement failing its test by hypocritically and blindly supporting a man that is completely antithetical to the values they espouse, but they are willing to use him to hold on to political power and protect them from imagined persecution to the point of believing election lies and attempting to overthrow the same government they hold as sacred. Conservative columnist Jennifer Rubin was appalled by this and was one of the few conservative voices willing to stand up and call it out:

> "I watched in horror in 2016 as Republicans embraced a racist bully bent on undermining our democracy and promoting White Christians' quest for political dominance. I witnessed one conservative "intellectual" and "respectable" publication after another deny, then rationalize, then defend and then laud a detestable figure who repudiated principles and positions that once animated them."
>
> "I saw social conservatives who demonized Bill Clinton swoon at the feet of a serial liar, adulterer and racist whose cruelty became a central feature of his presidency. Republicans who once insisted character was a critical factor in selecting leaders seemed almost giddy when Trump unleashed his personal viciousness on their progressive opponents."[2]

I have been told that this is all acceptable because "God chose a flawed leader, but the one we need for the moment", all because he pays lip service to them and knows he can play them all for fools in order to hold on to his power. They are willing to accept a corrupt bargain, and as my wife recently told me, "I don't trust a politician that tells me how to pray or a religious person who tells me how to vote." She is smarter than me, so I should listen to her more.

It is not limited to that side either, as you have those in power to affect real, significant change for good in the world but refuse to do so because it might affect their wallets, their power, or their standing. Look at Joe Manchin and Kyrsten Sinema, who are personally holding up a wealth of

---

2. Rubin, Jennifer—How Trump Mobilized Women, Including Me—*The Washington Post*—https://www.washingtonpost.com/opinions/2021/09/20/jennifer-rubin-republican-trump-resistance/

legislation that can do some real good not only in this country in terms of voting rights, social assistance, and more, but also in the world in terms of fighting climate change. It would be funny if it were not so tragic that the Evangelical right fears a socialist takeover by the Democratic Party when the Democratic Party can't even agree what it wants to do while it has the power to do that.

Finally, you have people that have been so downtrodden by those in power or those that have railed against them that there is no longer any compassion or empathy when their opponents suffer or even die.

We really are a broken world that is failing tests, but it is one so broken that we cannot even see how deeply broken we are. There is always a chance to do better, even if it means doing better in those smaller moments. It is going to take personal sacrifice and it has to begin on a base level. I lack the power to change legislation, end poverty, or combat injustice on a global scale. I can at least try to impact my own little corner of the world.

This book would not exist if not for one of my own largest tests. During my first year of college, I was very unsure of what I wanted to do. I was unsure if I had even picked the right school. I was going to college because it was the next thing expected of me. I started as an athletic training major because I had a love of sports and knew I wanted to work in that field, but being a professional athlete was not going to happen.

In the first month of college I switched to Communications, but I wasn't sure if it was right. I went to my classes, got good grades, and did the college thing, but I missed my friends and would often return home on weekends since I lived only an hour away. I didn't know what I wanted to do by the end of that first year and I even pondered leaving school and coming home to do . . . I don't even know what.

One weekend in late March of my first year I was home and went to dinner with my parents. I expressed this wanderlust to them and how I was unsure of what to do. My father, a man of great wisdom, told me to trust my instincts and to not be afraid of deciding. His exact words were, "God's not going to come up, slap you in the face with a fish, and tell you to go be a fisherman."

The next day I had my first real positive "college experience" when the women's basketball team for Purdue University won the national championship. I got to enjoy one of the most festive nights on campus as we celebrated the accomplishment. That convinced me that I should stay in school instead of moping about not wanting to be there.

This is Only a Test

Then came the metaphorical fish.

Back in Chapter 5 I mentioned my first trip to Wrigley Field with my grandfather. It is one of my favorite childhood memories because I used to watch Cubs games on WGN with him every summer. It was our time to bond, and when he took me to Wrigley that first time it was incredible seeing everything in person. Even in my 40s I still shed a tear every time I walk up the steps to see the ivy.

That trip would be memorable in more ways than one. It was put on by my small-town newspaper. They got a block of tickets, chartered a pair of motorcoaches, and sold them to people in town one day a year to head up and see the Cubs. The staff of the sports department was on the bus, and one of the editors was amazed that I, only 8 at the time, knew so much about sports and the Cubs.

This same editor was still working at the paper 11 years later when I was in school when I came across his path again. I don't remember exactly how, but he remembered me as that kid that knew all the sports stuff. I told him I was studying communications at Purdue and he asked me if I would be willing to come on as a stringer, covering high school sports and other local events.

That was in April of 1999. I got my first byline the next month, writing a story on a youth baseball tournament. From there I was hooked. While I would bounce around and do a lot of jobs related to writing, I knew that was supposed to write in at least some capacity from that moment. It was that fish moment.

To this day I still write for that paper from time to time because I have always love Indiana high school basketball and it is great to get paid for a hobby. It eventually led to me starting my own Purdue sports blog, which took off and now has thousands of readers all over the country (and even the world since I have gotten emails from as far away as Argentina about a former Purdue player playing basketball down there). It even led to this book because of the time and hours I have put into writing and honing a craft until now.

All of this came out of being tested and being willing to learn from those tests. I didn't know what I wanted to do, but I was tested to figure it out. Along the way there was compassion and encouragement. There was my grandfather and his love for me that took me to Wrigley Field that day. There were my parents, encouraging me to not give up. There was David Kasey and Dave Kitchell, giving a 19-year-old kid a chance to write about

Compassion

sports for the first time. There was my wife encouraging me to start my own thing when I was struggling to get noticed for other jobs. There was my early blog audience, that at least enjoyed what I wrote enough to tell their friends about it and grow the audience.

It is also my responsibility to pay this kindness and compassion back by being the same type of mentor that I needed. My Purdue blog it is now large enough that I have a staff of wonderful guys that share my same passion for writing irreverently about Purdue sports. I have known these guys a long time and I have seen them tested as well, but we lift each other up. In the past two years two of my writers have become fathers for the first time. That is an enormous test, of course. I have been happy to provide them encouragement and what wisdom I have, mainly that the first step to being a decent parent is admitting that you will never once even come close to figuring it all out. In turn, they have become part of my own support system through even more tests.

I have even gotten a chance to return the favor that David Kasey and Dave Kitchell did for me a long time ago by helping another young writer get his first shot. In late 2019 a young 20-year-old Purdue student by the name of Jace Jellison contacted me about writing for our site. I needed a student on campus that could cover events as well as someone who could fulfill the role of covering women's basketball for us. Jace took it and ran with it, and has become a great voice for our audience. He has covered some men's basketball games for us, and the joy on his face that I saw when he posted a picture of standing on the court at Mackey Arena wearing our media badge made me feel like a proud dad because I could give him a chance and because I remember when I got to cover my first big event.

In turn, he has been able to grow his own brand with a successful podcast that has had multiple Purdue sports celebrities on it. Our name gave his podcast more legitimacy, and his hard work has paid off as he created his own thing. I could not be prouder.

I would have not passed my first major test leading me to this day if not for the kindness and compassion of those before me. It is, therefore, my responsibility to return that favor by showing kindness and compassion to others so that they can pass their own tests and seize the opportunities given to them. Maybe in the long run it will have a larger effect.

13

Love in the Time of Screaming Hot Takes

BEING BLUNT IS NOT a development born out of my adulthood. It has been around for a while. When I was a sophomore in high school it was the first time I seriously looked into dating. It helped that I had just gotten my driver's license, which in central Indiana with nothing but cornfields around is a big deal. I started dating a freshman for a few weeks around Christmas. It was a fun little relationship, but nothing too serious. It was also the middle of basketball season.

High school basketball in Indiana is diminished today, but it is still a near religion the state takes very seriously. In the mid-90s, before our beloved state tournament was ruined, it was even more serious. I grew up going to every high school game, home or away, and when I was in elementary school the local players were idols, especially since my sister, who is nine years older than I, had classes with them. I can still tell you virtually every detail about the team that made the 1989 state championship game to this day.

By the time I was in high school it was apparent I was not going to be the player on the team I dreamed of being, but I still wanted to help, so I became a student manager just to be part of it. This was in the middle of said relationship, so it was a busy time. I had to be at practice most nights and weekends often meant Friday and Saturday games. After a while, the girl I was dating tried to give me an ultimatum: Did I love her more or basketball?

Compassion

Well, it was 1996 and our team was undefeated and ranked No. 1 in the state with a chance to win it all. It was a no brainer. Without blinking I said, "basketball," thus ending the relationship. It was a disappointing end, and basketball would have a disappointing end, as we only lost one game in the regular season but were upset in the round of 16 in the state tournament.

It has been more than 25 years since that moment, but I still remember it clearly. It was a lesson in compassion and how it relates to love. Was I in love with that girl and did I miss out on a lifelong romance? Both were extremely unlikely. I was 16 and she was 15, but at the time I am sure it was a big deal. I didn't exactly show a lot of compassion and it ended over a silly game that I and few others remember the details of.

Love is perhaps the ultimate expression of compassion. I know that is something cliché that sounds like it should be on a Hallmark card but think about it for a moment. We are most compassionate with those we love. We have the most patience for those we love (probably because they test that patience the most). We have the most empathy for those we love. Love is something we fight for. It is something that causes us to overlook flaws, mistakes, and even pain regardless of the type of love. While this is far from a comprehensive list, here are some of the different types of love I see:

- **Romantic Love**—This is what we have for our spouses and significant others. It is the type of love that changes our worldviews and makes us commit to do anything for the other person.
- **Familial Love**—We're legally obligated to love these people by blood, even if we don't like them at times.
- **Parental Love**—Not only do we fight to protect and love our kids, but we also want to teach them, so they don't make the same mistakes we have. They are the pieces of ourselves we send into the future.
- **Friendly Love**—We love the people we have shared experiences with over the long haul. We appreciate their companionship and, and it can grow into Romantic Love under the right conditions.
- **Faithful Love**—This is the love we have for God and matters of faith. They are what shapes our attitudes and the beliefs we fight for.

There are other types of love out there, too. I love my cat because she is a wonderful companion, and she helped all three of us in my immediate family by showing up on our porch at the right time. I love Purdue basketball because of the thrill it gives me to be in a deafening Mackey Arena even though it certainly does not love me back every mid-to-late March. I love having the sunroof in my car so I can drive with loud music back from covering a high school football game on a late summer night.

Part of love is sacrifice. It is impossible to love without putting at least part of yourself below someone or something else. I can't love my cat without being able to spend the money for vet visits and pet supplies. I can't love Purdue basketball without a foreboding sense of dread around March 15th every year. In love that stems from personal relationships we sacrifice much, mostly because we expect that sacrifice and love in return. It is part of an unspoken contract.

Jesus made the ultimate sacrifice out of love. We are always told this in Sunday school, but He had a lot to say about the topic even before He went to the Cross. Here are some of the things Jesus said about love (all very much paraphrased):

- God loved the world, so He gave His Son so we wouldn't perish.—John 3:16
- You should love the Lord your God with all your might.—Matthew 22:37
- As the Father loved me, so I should love you.—John 15:9
- There is no greater love than laying down your life for your friends—John 15:13
- Love one another.—John 13:34, also in John 15:12
- Love your enemies.—Matthew 5:43

The Gospel of John is basically an entire book on Jesus speaking of different types of love, but His actions in the other gospels also spoke. He loved Lazarus and wept bitterly at his death. He loved children. He loved His followers. He told us that love was His most important commandment in the Gospel of Mark. He loved strangers. He loved outcasts. He loved the crippled and lame. He even called us to love our enemies and those who persecute us. If you have been paying attention in the last five years, that is something that is not happening. Love is supposed to be a unifying force, but we are anything but unified and it is clear that things are getting worse.

In his letter to the Ephesians Paul spoke explicitly about the need for unity and maturity within the body of Christ:

Compassion

> "As a prisoner for the Lord, then, I urge you to live a life worthy of the calling you have received. [2] Be completely humble and gentle; be patient, bearing with one another in love. [3] Make every effort to keep the unity of the Spirit through the bond of peace. [4] There is one body and one Spirit, just as you were called to one hope when you were called; [5] one Lord, one faith, one baptism; [6] one God and Father of all, who is over all and through all and in all."—Ephesians 4:1–6

We live in an era of hot takes, Twitter bon mots, and screaming heads. Unity in anything feels like a pipe dream as we cannot get anyone to agree that something is universally right or wrong. In Paul's time he had started several churches across the eastern Mediterranean and even then, they had their differences. Just look in the first two chapters of Revelation. Each of the churches mentioned is called out on their shortcomings.

The church in Ephesus is said to have forsaken the love it had at first. The church in Smyrna is called afflicted and poor. The church in Pergamum is said to have followed other teachings apart from Christ, thus leading followers astray. The church in Thyatira is said to lead people into sexual immorality. The church in Sardis is told to "wake up because their deeds are unfinished in the sight of God". The church in Philadelphia is said to have little strength. Finally, the church in Laodicea is called lukewarm, thus lacking conviction.

When you read the descriptions of these churches in Revelation, they read like one- and two-star Yelp reviews. They also represent the flaw that humanity brings to the church. This is maybe 50 years at best after Christ's time. Many who witnessed His ministry firsthand were still alive and had been involved in the planting of these churches, yet already the story was being changed by human hands and perspectives. Now here we are, 2,000 years later, and we rely on translations of translations of tattered letters and oral stories passed down.

I am not saying that the Bible itself is therefore wrong because of it, but it is impossible to not look at it without seeing the perspectives of not only the authors of each book, but those that translated it and assembled it centuries ago. It does represent a certain unity in overall messages and viewpoints, but even then, there are modern day arguments such as "only this translation is correct and all others are wrong", usually to make a point that backs up their specific worldview. In the end, it is impossible to have a 100% accurate depiction of what was written nearly 2,000 years ago.

Love in the Time of Screaming Hot Takes

What stands out about those "Yelp reviews" laid down by John at the beginning of Revelation is that they come from a place of compassion. The underlying message is, "Guys, you've wandered off from the message this way. I want to you to get back on track!" Even in his criticism he is complementary, like he said to the church in Laodicea:

> "Those whom I love I rebuke and discipline. So be earnest and repent. 20 Here I am! I stand at the door and knock. If anyone hears my voice and opens the door, I will come in and eat with that person, and they with me."—Revelation 3:19–20

I think this is why I struggle so much with many members of the church today in America. I see their actions and how they come in conflict with the values they espouse, and it stings because it comes from people that have meant so much in my life. I know they come to their positions earnestly but are influenced by the communities they keep around them. The same is true for me. We both follow the same God and work with the same source material in the Bible, but the unity is not there, even when there is that connection of love. I see these communities as increasingly inflexible because they deny basic, good faith evidence to different views.

Because I am not perfect, I am guilty of turning away from that love, be it familial, friendly, parental, or even sometimes faithful. I do not have a prefect world view. I don't think that I am some sort of prophet that has it all figured out and can fix things with some magical words, but I am also cautious of anyone else who thinks they do have that magical secret. I often bring my own shovelfuls of coal to stoke the hot take furnace, and it is often out of anger and not compassion.

We are called to unity though, and to me, that unity comes through compassion. It comes through patience. It comes through a willingness to step outside of our bubbles and accept that maybe we might be wrong about some things, large or small, with a healthy dose of humility. I know I have said it a lot, but it must start on a small scale. I did not have a grand idea that starting this book was going to unite the world in some sort of magical utopia. I began writing it because I saw the broken relationships and bitter anger in the world even at a personal level and I wanted to speak up about it. I wanted to say that we can do better, and it begins in these smaller relationships. As much as I want to rain fire with my anger, I know I can accomplish more with a quiet, thoughtful word, probably because people who know me would expect the wrathful anger part first.

Compassion

Hot takes don't increase love. They do not call for unity. If you're reading this from outside the U.S., believe me. We just had four years of a Presidency built solely on hot takes. It is not fun. They are meant to be divisive and rile us up. It reminds me of the one panel comic where a man is sitting at his computer and yells to his wife in the other room, "Not now, someone is wrong on the internet!" I have yet to meet a person who has won an internet argument, and there are days where I am still not smart enough to avoid an internet argument. It is a place where what you say not only can be used against you, but it WILL also be used against you, even if you said it 12 years ago.

The hot take culture we live in goes against everything that Christ taught us about humility. The value of taking a moment to pause and think before responding simply won't be tolerated in this space. Even the calls for unity that we are asked to do go ignored.

It all goes back to that attitude of "Do Something". Yes, we know that God is in control. He runs the entire universe and everything in it. We still have a role to play. We are not robots twirling away on a path to predestination (unless you're a Calvinist, in which case, have at it). It is very clear in the Gospels that Christ calls us to do our part. We are to love. We are to work together to at least try to achieve unity. We are to support each other. It starts small with our own individual relationships because that is all we really can control. We must do the small things, and trust that God has all the big things covered. I cannot begin to fathom what the mind of God is like, so I cannot begin to fathom what overall unity is. All I can do is fulfill the role I am supposed to have and let Him handle the rest. Even then, finding that role for myself is difficult, and we can only do our best.

14

Forgive Even When You Can't Forget

REMEMBER THE STORY I told of my grandmother in Chapter 4 on being selfish and selfless with grace? I have learned that her inability to forgive and forget is hereditary. I loved her very much, but she was an expert at holding a grudge. She had a hard time forgiving people who had wronged her and that is a lesson I have also struggled with in adulthood. My inability to forgive has often led to simmering resentment, which then manifests itself into bitterness. That bitterness then evolves into a brooding darkness.

There is a subtle difference between grace and forgiveness. Grace is often defined as divine assistance or sanctification. It can also mean approval or favor. Grace is given to us freely through Christ's sacrifice on the Cross, but we can also provide grace to others without being wronged. Grace is a form of patience. We have grace when our children are learning a new skill or testing our patience with their actions. We have grace when things are not going our way, as we look forward to another day to try again.

Forgiveness is different. Forgiveness doesn't come unless an offense is committed. It is an action. It is a choice. We know that something wrong has been done, but we seek to cease resentment. Even regarding debt there is a difference between grace and forgiveness. A grace period is given to give more time to repay a debt. Forgiveness means the debt is no more, regardless of the amount of payment left.

The fact that forgiveness requires a choice makes it more difficult. There is real pain when we are wronged, and in that pain, we want to seek

Compassion

justice. It is human nature to want to deny forgiveness even as we are called to forgive. We want people to feel the pain we are feeling, not walk away scot free with no consequences for their actions. It gets even worse when we live in a culture where you can get away scot free if you have the money and power to do so.

Just as we need God's grace for our own salvation, we need forgiveness here in this life to maintain personal relationships. Think about the person you have known the longest in your life. Has there ever been a time where you have had to forgive them for something, large or small? Just like we as human beings are not perfect, all interpersonal relationships are not perfect.

I gave an example of this back in the second chapter when I had a major falling out with some of my closest friends and walked away for a time. Eventually, when I grew up a little and came back to the group, they were kind enough to forgive me. I have known many of these people since middle school, if not before, and even though the responsibilities of adulthood mean that we don't get to see each other very often, they are some of my biggest supporters. This stems from both the grace they had to let me grow past my mistakes and the forgiveness they offered for my actions.

Even while writing this book one of the principal people involved in that incident provided the biggest encouragement. During the first home game of Purdue's 2021 football season, I was able to meet up with the hosts of a podcast I appeared on for our opponent, Oregon State. I posted the picture on Facebook, marveling over the fact that a blog I had started with no audience more than 15 years ago now had people looking at me as an expert, so much so that people from the other side of the country wanted me on their show to share my opinions. It makes me feel like a Q list celebrity. This friend of mine simply said, "I am so proud of you . . . I am not sure that I have ever said that. I am glad you kept writing."

She is not a sports fan. She has had her differences with me over more than 25 years of friendship, and some of those differences were very loud. These differences didn't matter. She saw past my poor choices and, to be quite honest, immaturity as a 19-year-old, and offered her forgiveness to mend the friendship. She was there for some of my nascent writings and wanted to offer encouragement both then and now. She was there at the beginning of my journey and encouraged me to take those first steps. She didn't have to do that. What I did directly affected her and was quite hurtful, but in the end the friendship we had, and the entire group of us had, was more important.

Forgive Even When You Can't Forget

Forgiveness has two sides though. First, the aggrieved side must be ready and willing to forgive. Second, you must be ready to accept forgiveness. I have long been my own harshest critic. For many mistakes in my past, I carried an attitude of, "they might forgive me, but I never will." That trait was one of many demons I dealt with for years, and I still feel its pull from time to time.

It is hard to describe it. I believe in being responsible for your own actions, but internally, this trait is on steroids when it comes to my own problems. I will heap all blame on myself, but I will also blame myself for other people's shortcomings when something goes wrong. My self-talk tells me that if it wasn't for my mistakes and my decisions, the person that screwed up would not have been able to screw up, so clearly it was my fault that something bad happened.

Messed up, isn't it?

It is not a fun way to live. It leads to bitterness and resentment towards ourselves. Trust me when I say that it causes more problems than it solves. I thought that by holding on to my pain like that, by acutely remembering every little detail of the situation, I could prevent worse things from happening it the future. Instead, it led to more fractured relationships, a cold nature, bitterness, and resentment.

Few external factors helped this either, as I fell into anxiety, depression, and even apathy. I would take medication for anxiety and depression, but after a while it was something I did because I was supposed to. I didn't realize that it was doing more harm than good until I finally tried to make a change. In my head I had the simple equation of, "I am taking the first medication I tried, so it must work and I need it" without realizing that it was not that simple. It took me more than 10 years to try something new and realize that tamping down my emotions and being numb was not a productive answer.

Bitterness and resentment became old friends, and they come from a lack of forgiveness towards ourselves or towards others. It doesn't matter who the beneficiary of forgiveness is. Until we are willing to offer it, it will only eat at us, and what does that accomplish? I have more than a decade of experience in seeing that bitterness and resentment solve nothing. They don't hurt the ones that have hurt us, either.

In Paul's letter to the Ephesians he speaks of why we need to get rid of anger:

Compassion

"Get rid of all bitterness, rage, anger, harsh words, and slander, as well as all types of evil behavior. Instead, be kind to each other, tenderhearted, forgiving one another, just as God through Christ has forgiven you."—Ephesians 4:31–32

This message is for our attitudes towards ourselves as well as towards others. That bitterness and resentment only poisons us. We must be willing to forgive and seek a way to move on, no matter how difficult that may be.

Of course, there is another side to that, and that is *accepting* forgiveness, which is another area I struggled with because I often felt like it was undeserved. It takes a lot to come to a place where we seek forgiveness for our actions, but the damage caused by said actions can lead to trouble with people accepting said forgiveness. Minor slights can be easily forgiven, but major slights cause deep scars that take a while to heal. Even once they have healed, what caused them is not forgotten.

That is why I called this chapter "Forgiving Even When You Can't Forget". Try as we might, forgetting major pain is probably not going to happen. Here is what Dr. Gregg Jantz had to say about forgiving without forgetting:

> "Some things cannot be mitigated. They cannot be fixed. They cannot be removed. They can only be forgiven. Forgiveness isn't a feeling. It is a strategic, purposeful response to pain and injury—one that can be acted on even if you don't feel like it. For some things, only the healing waters of forgiveness have the power to douse the flames of anger. Extending forgiveness is one of the hardest things to do in life. Yet, it brings you closer to the character of God."[1]

Just as offering forgiveness is an act of compassion and a purposeful action, acting on that forgiveness is a purposeful choice. It is harder to forgive those that are not seeking forgiveness, but it often needs to be done to move forward. Accepting offered forgiveness is easier, but the person seeking forgiveness still needs to prove their intent with actions, sometimes for quite a while, to truly earn it. Forgiveness does not mean freedom from consequences, as Silverio Gonzalez says:

> "Of course, there are natural consequences in this world. Having sex outside of marriage produces children outside of marriage. When people break the civil law, they have to deal with civil authorities. People sometimes must suffer the natural consequence

---

1. Dr. Jantz, Gregory—How to Forgive Without Forgetting—*A Place of Hope*—https://www.aplaceofhope.com/how-to-forgive-without-forgetting/

of sin in this world, but we don't add to their misery by making them pay a debt to us. Forgiveness means that we shoulder the burden of their debt to us."[2]

Facing consequences even when forgiven is not always a negative, as long as you're open to learning from those trials. They can be hard lessons. Consequences are still important because without them, poor behavior goes unchecked. Unless we're willing to learn hard lessons from the consequences we face it will not lead to necessary changed behavior. A little pain now will save a lot of pain later.

It is why it is important to have these discussions with our children from a young age. Teaching these lessons early is yet another form of compassion. These lessons are taught out of love because we want our children to thrive, but it can be hard on the parents as well. I refuse to let my son grow up as some entitled brat that thinks consequences and rules do not apply to him. It is difficult, but necessary to establish that I forgive him for his mistakes, but he still must face those lessons and learn from them.

Jesus spoke a lot about forgiveness. Remember the story of the crippled man in Matthew 9:

> "[2] Some men brought to him a paralyzed man, lying on a mat. When Jesus saw their faith, he said to the man, "Take heart, son; your sins are forgiven.""
>
> "[3] At this, some of the teachers of the law said to themselves, "This fellow is blaspheming!'"
>
> "[4] Knowing their thoughts, Jesus said, "Why do you entertain evil thoughts in your hearts? [5] Which is easier: to say, 'Your sins are forgiven,' or to say, 'Get up and walk'? [6] But I want you to know that the Son of Man has authority on earth to forgive sins." So he said to the paralyzed man, "Get up, take your mat and go home." [7] Then the man got up and went home."—Matthew 9:2–7

This was such a revolutionary attitude at the time. The religious leaders of His day had a monopoly on how sins could be forgiven. There is an entire manual in the Old Testament on the sacrifices and rituals that needed to be performed to atone for sin, so by simply saying, "your sins are forgiven," Jesus was basically committing blasphemy against the established religious leaders. This is even before you consider how He was cutting into the racket they had going on in the Temple. Do you know how long it takes

---

2. Gonzalez, Silverio—*Forgive Like Jesus*—*Core Christianity*—*https://corechristianity.com/resource-library/articles/forgive-like-jesus/*

Compassion

to find two perfect, unblemished doves for a sacrifice? It is a lot easier to buy right there at the temple.

They could not fathom someone simply forgiving sins, especially since it detracted from the power that they held in the Temple. If Jesus could forgive sins with a word, what did the religious elite, the gatekeepers of their faith, then have? Instead of being open to change or accept new ideas, they did everything they can to stomp out this threat to their power. That doesn't sound familiar with anything going on today, does it?

Which is easier: forgiveness or judgement? Which plays more to our human desires: forgiveness and being accommodating to someone else's human-ness, or judgement and insisting we are in the right?

Forgiveness involves a healthy dose of humility, but it is another path to compassion. When we forgive, we admit that we were wronged, but we are willing to move forward for the benefit of someone else at the cost of our own feelings. When we forgive, we follow one of the most essential traits that Jesus exhibited. Jesus came to forgive as well as act as an arbiter for us. All are under the condemnation of God, but the sacrifice of Jesus means we will not face that condemnation. It was His act, not our own, that grants us forgiveness.

This is on a grand cosmic scale and not within our interpersonal relationships. Jesus is the Son of God, set higher than any man and is someone not seen every day. Even though we act in prayer, study the Word, and work to increase our faith, He is not someone we sit down with at work and have a meeting with. He is not at the dinner table after a long day as we try to avoid an argument with a family member because we're irritable from something that occurred at work.

Trying to practice forgiveness on either side is more difficult in the real world. It is what we are supposed to do, sure, but when you see someone's face or even hear their name their words and actions come back in full force. The worse their actions, the harder it is. I am still angry at Zach Randolph for his role in ending my high school basketball season my senior year with an overtime loss, but that pales in comparison to the real hurt others feel. Think of the parents who lost children in a school shooting, or someone who loses a loved one to a drunk driver. Those situations make it difficult to find forgiveness, and I even empathize with those people that can't get to that point. It feels justified.

I have been there. It wasn't Zach Randolph, but I carried around a deep bitterness and resentment for many years towards someone who deeply wronged me. I can't go into details because it is far too personal, but it was part of a terrible time and it burned me emotionally. It was a mental cancer. It ate at me for more than 10 years even though I may have seen them three times in that period. I seethed at the mere thought of this person, coming up with elaborate mental scenarios for revenge that I would never carry out, but for some reason my brain thought it would make me feel better.

What did it accomplish though? What good did my simmering rage do? It only fueled my innate bitterness, made me even more distant and closed off emotionally. It made me push away those who cared about me the most. It made me damaged for a very long time, and in that damage, I caused more to those around me. It is damage that I am still trying to dig out of, and I will probably be digging out of it for some time.

The point is that I finally did forgive. This person will never know it, as I don't really interact with them, but I finally came to terms and forgave them. I also, and this was significantly harder, forgave myself. I forgave myself for being captive to my own bitterness. I forgave myself for the role I played in everything. Most importantly, I forgave myself just for being myself.

Forgiveness is hard. It takes a lot of compassion to be forgive. It also gives a lot back, which is like why the word "give" is in there.

15

The Difference Between Knowledge and Wisdom

As a big Star Wars fan, I love each piece of the saga in its own way. I waited anxiously for the prequels, went to the midnight viewing for all of them, and after years of seeing them ebb and flow in esteem from the fandom, I even have a certain appreciation for them. Yes, even Attack of the Clones.

It is in Attack of the Clones that one character has a line that will end up being the basis for this chapter. Dexter Jettster, a creature called a Besalisk who has four arms and who runs a diner, appears in just one scene. It is when Obi-Wan Kenobi goes to him to analyze a dart that was used to kill a character in an earlier scene. Obi-Wan, with all the knowledge of the Jedi at his fingertips in the temple, cannot identify where the unique weapon was from, so he turned to his friend Dexter.

Dexter identifies it as a Kamino Saberdart, all from taking a quick look at it and noticing a small, but critical detail that sets it apart:

> "It's these funny little cuts on the side that give it away. Those analysis droids only focus on symbols. Huh! I should think that you Jedi would have more respect for the difference between knowledge and . . . heh heh heh . . . wisdom."[1]

---

1. Star Wars Episode II: Attack of the Clones—Lucasfilm Ltd.

The Difference Between Knowledge and Wisdom

If we're going to live compassionately, knowing the difference between knowledge and wisdom is critical. In life we can acquire a lot of knowledge, but without wisdom, it can be useless. I look at wisdom as the ability to apply knowledge correctly. It is the ability to have good judgement. It is the ability to discern things. It is the ability to conclude and decide based on experience, judgement, and, yes, knowledge. Knowledge is just one component of wisdom. It is valuable, but using knowledge correctly requires wisdom.

I'll give you an example. One of the best Purdue basketball players of the last 25 years was Carsen Edwards. He was one of the most unique players we had in that he could create his own shot from pretty much anywhere on the floor. He was quick, a good shooter, a solid ballhandler, and he carried a confidence about him that is a huge asset on the basketball court. It was not uncommon for him to pull up a few steps after crossing half court and shoot because he was just feeling it. In terms of knowledge, I could tell you his three-point shooting percentage. I could tell you if her preferred to drive to the basket with his right or left hand. I could tell you that you had to be careful because he could, and would, shoot from anywhere. These are facts gathered from studying his game on film and watching him play for three seasons.

That's a lot of knowledge. In terms of wisdom though, coaches, opponents, and even Carsen himself had to have a certain amount of wisdom from these skills and stats to use said knowledge properly. Coach Matt Painter had to know how to use him properly in the lineup to maximize the team's success. Carsen was guy shooting 15–20 times per game. That can be about 40% of a team's shots, so how does that factor in with the other four players on the floor? For opponents, how do you find a way to defend him? For Carsen himself, how did he know to harness his incredible God-given abilities? How did he see the game as it was happening, with 10 moving parts, and know within a split second just when to shoot, drive, or pass?

All of this comes from time, experience, knowledge, and judgement. Wisdom is something that rarely comes immediately. It is granted over time, that the experience component of it. "Listen to advice and accept instruction, that you may gain wisdom in the future." Says Proverbs 19:20. Yes, knowledge is a critical component of wisdom, but so is time, patience, experience, humility, and, yes, compassion. Instruction provides knowledge in the moment, but wisdom is how you apply said knowledge.

At 42 I am wiser than I was at 22, but in no way would I consider myself wise. I will very likely be even wiser when I am 62 as I am now. If I am

Compassion

lucky enough to make it to 82 who knows what wisdom I will have gained. The more open we are to gaining wisdom the more we will gain it, as well. It takes an open mind and being willing to admit when we are wrong to maximize what we can learn.

No one's wisdom is completely infallible. Tony Bennett is one of the best coaches in the country. His Virginia teams run a stifling defense and it is common for them to hold opponents under 50 points. He has established one of the best basketball programs in America that specializes in stopping you defensively, and he has a smart mind that can figure out several teams. He was still lucky to beat Purdue on a night where Carsen scored 42 points, hit 10 threes, and was burying shots 35 feet from the basket. Carsen took his best laid plans and set them on fire just by shooting over his famous "pack line" defense that thrives on protecting everything inside the three-point arc. He was red hot, especially in the second half, and Virginia had no answer. Bennett has a wealth of knowledge, experience, and wisdom about basketball. Carsen baffled his entire team that night by having the game of his life and almost beating them single-handedly, and they barely escaped on a 1-in-100 play at the end of regulation to force overtime.

Even in that play there was an application of wisdom that did not work out. With a little over five seconds left Purdue was leading by three points and Virginia had the basketball. A year earlier Purdue was in the same situation playing Tennessee, and it chose not to foul on purpose. The Volunteers hit a tying three, the game went to overtime, and Tennessee eventually won. You wouldn't normally foul intentionally while leading, but the idea is that if you foul with five seconds or less on the clock you can only give up two points at the free throw line instead of a potential game-tying three. From his experience previously, coach Painter elected to try something new and chose to foul.

Unfortunately, it backfired here too. Virginia hit the first free throw and missed the second intentionally. The ball was batted far into the backcourt and Kehei Clark gathered the batted rebound. With the clock running, facing the wrong way, and with the basketball 60 feet from the basket Clark had the ball, but it still looked like the game was won for Purdue. Clark turned and instead of panicking and firing up a desperation heave he roped a laser of a pass to Mamadi Diakite. He caught the ball and got a shot off over the 7'2" Matt Haarms with less than half a second left, hitting the tying basket as time expired in a wild play that broke my heart.

The Difference Between Knowledge and Wisdom

Coach Painter had a good, sound strategy and a great application of wisdom. It made perfect sense that with little time on the clock and a three point lead you foul to make it extremely difficult for the team to get the three points they need. It wasn't infallible, all because Clark had the wisdom to see his teammate and pass for a better shot instead of throwing up a desperate heave. We are fallible in everything we do. It still doesn't mean we don't try our best to apply the wisdom we have based on our experiences and circumstances.

Buddhist lama Khandro Rinpoche has said,

> "The human heart is basically very compassionate, but without wisdom, compassion will not work. Wisdom is the openness that lets us see what is essential and most effective."[2]

I am sure some Christians would immediately be on guard that this quote came from a non-Christian source, but if you've come this far you've already been through a discussion involving the movie *Dogma*, so this is nothing compared to that.

Wisdom is only one of the parts of compassion, and it is not infallible. What I mentioned above is only an example, but it was not a situation of grand importance. It was just a silly basketball game. It shows even when we do the right thing all the time it does not guarantee nothing bad will happen, and since we're human it is difficult to do the right thing every single time. By using the wisdom given us it does help us have an edge though.

When it comes to wisdom and compassion relating to each other I must once again turn to some Buddhist teachings. Dharma Master Cheng Yen states, "Wisdom is [knowing] the principles, and compassion is putting them into action. When compassion and wisdom converge, we will develop universal compassion. This is our goal." He then elaborates on this further:

> "In Tzu Chi, every day we walk the path of compassion. Motivated by love for others, we go to them to offer our aid and care. But, how can we help them in order to truly relieve their suffering? Where do we begin and how should we proceed? All this requires wisdom. To help others, we need to bring forth not only compassion but also wisdom.
>
> "Wisdom is like eyes that enable us to see. Wisdom, insight and understanding enable us to determine whether we're going

---

2. Stone, Tammy T.—Wisdom & Compassion: Why We Need Both to Be Fulfilled—*Elephant Journal*—https://www.elephantjournal.com/2014/11/wisdom-compassion-why-we-need-both-to-be-fulfilled/

Compassion

in the right direction. It is very easy to veer off the right path, and with the slightest change in direction our route will change quite significantly so we'll end up far off course."

"We need the eyes of wisdom to keep us on track. Along the way, there are also likely to be pitfalls and obstacles. Only with the vision provided by wisdom, insight and understanding can we successfully avoid these. While walking the path of compassion, we therefore need to be very alert."[3]

These are Buddhist-centered teachings, but they can apply to everyday life outside of Buddhism. This entire passage sounds like it could belong in the book of Proverbs, and we do see several similar examples there:

> "One who is wise is cautious and turns away from evil, but a fool is reckless and careless."—Proverbs 14:16

> "The beginning of wisdom is this: Get wisdom, and whatever you get, get insight."—Proverbs 4:7

> "Whoever trusts in his own mind is a fool, but he who walks in wisdom will be delivered."—Proverbs 28:26

> "Know that wisdom is such to your soul; if you find it, there will be a future, and your hope will not be cut off."—Proverbs 24:14

The Bible calls us to gain wisdom. This leads to discernment, from which we can properly apply so many other spiritual gifts including compassion. I go back to pastor Ryan Carrell of the Southeast Project in Indianapolis. In a recent sermon series on Paul's letter to the Ephesians he spoke strongly about wisdom and how it can be used when he quoted Andy Stanley, a pastor in Atlanta by saying, "In light of my past experience, my current circumstances, and my future hopes & dreams, what is the wise thing to do?" Pastor Stanley used it in his book *Ask it* in the following context:

> "This letter was written in the language of the people in Ephesus. The language they spoke was called Koine Greek which was the language of the common every day person in their community. The phrase in Greek that Paul, the author, uses here is ἀκριβῶς περιπατεῖτε."

> "The first word is where we get our word acrobat. The second word means walking which, in scripture, is a metaphor for life. Walk like an acrobat would walk, with agility and balance."

---

3. Tzu Chi USA—The Union of Wisdom & Compassion—https://tzuchi.us/blog/the-union-of-wisdom-and-compassion

The Difference Between Knowledge and Wisdom

"What Paul is saying is, if you want to live a life that you don't regret, you have to be completely aware of what's around you, what's ahead of you, and what's behind you. You have to balance all of those things. You have to be aware of the tension, and lean into it."

"The way to put this awareness in a succinct question would be like this:"

"In light of my past experience, my current circumstances, and my future hopes and dreams, what is the wise thing to do?"[4]

To me, that sounds very close to the Buddhist teaching above, only said in a Christian context. Also, it flies in the face of the Hot Take culture from chapter 13 because it is basically asking us to stop and think before we act so we can make sure we do the compassionate thing. Again, that is not easy.

I am a hothead. My nature is to fire off the hot takes, consequences be damned. Lately I have seen more of how that is not the compassionate thing to do. The wave of COVID deniers and anti-vaxxers getting sick and even dying is at its peak as I write this. I see it daily on Twitter, and my first reaction is often a, "Good. You deserve it. Bye." That defeats my entire premise of writing this book. If I am railing against the sheer disdain and lack of compassion from those on that side, how am I any better when I am indifferent or even celebratory when they face their comeuppance?

It has led me to feel a lot of guilt because I have to deal with my own emotions that are against the very subject I am writing about. Most days I have to put Twitter away or make sure I am just following only my sports community on there because otherwise I see how it poisons me and takes away from my own ability to feel compassion for others. It makes me the very hypocrite that I have come to oppose.

It's hard. It goes back to my belief that sometimes "I don't know" is okay. I also have to tell myself that perseverance has not finished its work in me, which is why James 1:4 has basically become a mantra.

This world can benefit from taking a deep breath and thinking for a moment. A pause is good. It is a small step, but an actionable one that once again falls under the "Do Something" category. Yes, a simple pause to think qualifies as doing something, because it allows us to collect ourselves and use the wisdom we're given. It lets us think of our past experience, our current circumstances, and future hopes and dreams to look at a situation more clearly so we can find the most compassionate response.

4. Stanley, Andy—*Ask It! The Question That Will Revolutionize How You Make Decisions*, Multnomah Press, 2014

Compassion

I haven't said much about prayer, but this is a great time to talk about it and its connection to wisdom. For a long time, I felt that prayer was a place where I had to say the right words to unlock its power and have my desires be answered. It was almost as if I needed to have a thesaurus next to me as I prayed, looking for the right synonym to unlock the proper praise to get a Godly, "yes". Even after I learned that sometimes God says, "no" because He's God and has a wider plan in mind I still thought prayer needed to have some flowery language out of respect.

Now I see prayer differently, and it has helped me understand wisdom a little better. If you can pray and have an audible conversation with God where He answers back, that's great. I am happy for you and hey, He's God. If He wants to do that, He can. I haven't been able to experience that, but my prayer life has evolved into a much more raw and cathartic experience. I pour myself into it, even when I feel like I might just be talking at my ceiling. If I am mad, I even let God know it. He's heard worse, I am sure. If I am flustered or distracted and don't really know what I am talking about He is fine with it. He also knows I am human and imperfect (and it's His fault because he made me that way).

At worst, prayer can be used as a quiet time to pause and reflect on what we have experienced, where we are, and where we're going to glean wisdom for . . . well, anything. I may not hear an audible voice from the Creator, but more often than not I at least feel a modicum of peace in my heart that allows me to focus. It is a calming, centering experience not unlike meditation.

It is another one of those smaller gestures that we can do that can compound into a larger effect. As one person, you can only do so much to change the world around you, but if your compassionate actions can change one other person's actions for the better, it can ripple into something larger. Therefore, we need to allow our wisdom to keep us on track. Christ wants us to pursue wisdom, as he said in Luke 21:15: "For I will give you a mouth and wisdom, which none of your adversaries will be able to withstand or contradict."

We're not going to be perfect. We're going to have moments where even our best efforts fall short, but those are chances to increase our wisdom from lived experience, and there is nothing wrong with that. It is true that when we are attempting to walk a path of compassion, as we are called to do, wisdom is essential. Even when we fail, we need to be open to it as a

The Difference Between Knowledge and Wisdom

learning experience, thus a chance to gain more wisdom so we can learn to act compassionately the next time.

16

Peace & Community Can Accomplish Greatness

Yeah, I am going to go to another basketball analogy. You can blame my mom for raising me in high school basketball gyms around the state of Indiana.

Mackey Arena is a throwback college basketball arena. At a little over 50 years old, it was renovated and improved a few seasons ago and will hopefully last another 50 years. Its official capacity is listed as 14,240, and when there is a game there it feels like 10 times that much. It features an old school metal roof, old bench seats for most of the seats, and it is designed as a perfect circle around the court with no angles, thus giving everyone roughly the same sightlines. It is perfect in its simplicity because there are few chairbacks, no luxury boxes, and few creature comforts, but there is a butt in every seat because the entire season sells out in minutes. Purdue knows that you're there to watch basketball, and the court is focus from every spot in the arena.

It is also very, very, VERY loud.

That metal roof serves a purpose. It reflects the sound directly back at the court, amplifying it with one entire quarter of the arena packed with thousands of screaming students. The basketball Sports Information Director Chris Forman has recorded a decibel level of 122.3 decibels on February 28, 2017 when Purdue beat Indiana to clinch its 23rd Big Ten

Peace & Community Can Accomplish Greatness

Championship[1]. That's the nearly equivalent of a jet engine. I was there that night, and it was loud, but I have been there other times before when I think it has been even louder.

Mackey is a special place. It reaches what I call "Saturn V Launch" levels of loud when Purdue really gets going, usually after a fast break dunk or big 3-pointer that caps a scoring run and has the opposing head coach jumping off the bench flailing his arms like he is trying to stop a runaway truck for a timeout because he knows the ref can't hear him. It reverberates through you in those moments, making you feel like you're about to burst, but in a good way.

I say that, because it is a place that myself and many others find peace, and that is such a compassionate blessing from God. In the 2020–21 season Purdue played with no fans. I watched every game on TV and did not get to attend a single one when I usually go several times per year. There were a few times where Purdue would go on those runs, but it would be deathly silent on the TV broadcast. It was so silent it was jarring, and I can only imagine it was worse in person. In fact, while this noise is often a tremendous home court advantage for Purdue (we rarely lose at Mackey of late), There is some mild concern that it might affect the *home* team in some seasons because the younger players on the team haven't played in front of these crowds yet. They do get used to it quickly though. In fact, coach Painter, when asked about crowd noise in other venues, has replied, "we play in Mackey Arena, so we're used to it."

There wasn't much peace watching something that has always been such a blessing. I am not alone in finding this loud maelstrom as a comfort. How is the beauty and compassion of God not seen in that? How do we not look at these moments, these shared experiences with strangers, and see a God that indeed does want us to be happy on this earth? It is not all judgments and condemnation and worship. He wants us to have these moments that we feel viscerally, where we have a connection to something larger than ourselves even if it is over something silly like a basketball game. It gives us even more reason to praise and worship Him in the end.

I had been looking forward to a return to Mackey for some time because of this. Then on November 27, 2021, my family and I were involved in a bad car accident. We were returning home from a football game when we had to stop due to slowed traffic in front of us. We had been stopped for maybe 2 seconds when we were hit from behind and pushed into the

---

1. https://twitter.com/purduesports/status/836792134908936192

Compassion

vehicle in front of us. All told, six vehicles were involved. A large SUV plowed into the car behind us to start the chain reaction, so we were the second car impacted.

Thankfully, my wife, son, and I were physically okay. We had some minor bumps and bruising and were sore for a few days, but our car was a total loss. Unfortunately, the driver of the vehicle pushed into us died and one of the passengers was seriously injured. This was a shock to all of us because there were no immediate signs that night of something serious. Once the first responders were on the scene there didn't seem to be any urgency that someone was in terrible distress, but two days later as I was settling everything with insurance and police, I was told the news.

It is something that stuck with me for a long time. Initially there was guilt. I thought I had stopped our car in time, but the moment of impact and the airbags deploying made a few critical seconds hazy. Had I really stopped? Was it my fault? Eventually the insurance companies informed me those other drivers said we stopped, but I still had doubts after receiving the awful news about the driver behind us. Even after our car's onboard computer data confirmed that yes, we were indeed at a complete stop upon impact, it is still something that bothered me for months. Someone had died and I was involved. Even though I wasn't at fault in any way it was haunting.

For months afterward I started having panic attacks, strangely when I would watch basketball games. I began to dread something that I have always loved. If the game was close my heart would start beating way too fast and my hands would shake. This was beyond normal "it's a close game" anxiety. These were full-fledged panic attacks. By January I couldn't even watch some of the games. We were in the middle of the most anticipated season in school history, and I was taking no joy from it. Even long after I had gotten over the worst of the fear of something happening while driving, I was still not able to sit and watch a basketball game.

Eventually my therapist determined that I had a form of PTSD that manifested itself when I watched games because we were returning from Purdue when the accident happened. She helped me begin a healing process that is still ongoing. Finally returning to Mackey in mid-February was part of it, as the fuel of the arena going full Saturn V launch loud after Sasha Stefanovic hit a big three during a 14–1 run felt like a balm to my soul. The game itself was still too close as Purdue only won by a point over an inferior team, but for a moment that afternoon 14,000 screaming fans due to Sasha hitting that one shot gave me more peace than I had experienced in months.

I see moments and places like this where compassion within community comes to the fore. I know I don't share the same societal, political, and faith views as everyone in Mackey Arena, but that seating bowl serves as a place where people united in one view can accomplish something great. We're there to will the Boilers on to wins, and we do our best to make opposing teams wilt in a dungeon of noise. Consequently, it gives us peace to be somewhere familiar with joyful memories compounding joyful memories. I have been going to that arena since I was a student, so I have nearly a quarter century of experiencing it at its very best. We were denied this as a comfort for over a year, and getting it back is just as praiseworthy as putting on worship music and lifting our hands in song. I see it as a gift from God.

I have also seen this diverse community do so much good. You may have heard of Purdue student Tyler Trent, a young man who was afflicted with a rare form of bone cancer that sadly took his life on January 1, 2019. He was only 20 years old, but when football coach Jeff Brohm found him and a friend camping out for the best seats outside of Ross-Ade Stadium the night before a September 2017 game against Michigan his story took off.

Tyler was uniquely blessed with an incredible positive attitude and deep peace about his illness. The morning before he went to camp out, he had been in Indianapolis for a chemotherapy treatment because of a recurrence of his cancer. In the next 16 months before his death, he worked for the school paper, followed the football and men's basketball teams all over the country, was featured on ESPN's College Gameday before Purdue upset No. 2 Ohio State on October 20, 2018, and became an inspiration for many around the country.

I admire him so much because it was never about him. Here was a young man that was dying, but he lived his Christian faith and worked tirelessly to raise several thousand dollars for childhood cancer research. Here is what the ESPN article on his passing had to say:

> "Millions of viewers learned about Trent's connection to the Boilermakers football team during the victory. In the two months that followed, he won the Disney Spirit Award and the Sagamore of the Wabash award, the highest civilian award given to Indiana citizens. He co-hosted an episode of SportsCenter. He wrote guest columns for the Indianapolis Star. A bobblehead doll was made in his likeness.

Compassion

Trent used his new platform to encourage donations to cancer research funds. The Tyler Trent Cancer Research Endowment raised more than $100,000. The bobblehead dolls also helped raise money for The V Foundation."[2]

I could say a lot more about what Tyler was able to accomplish. The larger point is that he did it in community, regardless of people's backgrounds, beliefs, views, or anything else. When there were more than 60,000 people in the stands for the Ohio State game and he was on the sidelines everyone was united. Even Ohio State fans in attendance proudly proclaimed, "CANCER SUCKS" at kickoff.

These moments of community give me peace, and they are something that gives me hope when there seem to be so few things to be hopeful for. Tyler's story is one of such overwhelming compassion in community. It was a community banding together to make a positive difference, but it was also Tyler's infinite compassion to do something with the little time he had left. Once the cancer had spread to his spine, he even voluntarily had a surgery to collect some of the cancer cells so they could be studied in the hopes they might provide a cure in the future. He knew it probably was not going to help him in the long run, but if it could help someone after him, he was all for it.

While Tyler has been gone for over three years, his story is still paying huge dividends because of the cells he donated:

> "The researchers found a variation in Trent's cells that has been found in tumors that recur, called the MYC-RAD21 signature. Lead researcher Dr. Karen Pollock says there are two drugs, a Chk1 inhibitor and a bromodomain inhibitor, that can block the effect of the variation. She says her team tested each one on Trent's cells individually and in combination.
>
> "What we found in Tyler's model is we can take one of these drugs, the Chk1 inhibitor or the bromodomain inhibitor, and we can administer it in models with the TT2 tumor and we get the tumors to stop growing some, compared to a control," Pollock says. "However, when we put the two drugs together, we block the growth of these tumors substantially.""[3]

---

2. Murphy, Dan—Tyler Trent, cancer patient who inspired many, dies at 20—https://twitter.com/purduesports/status/836792134908936192

3. Benson, Darian—Tyler Trent's Cells Lead to Groundbreaking Therapy—https://www.wfyi.org/news/articles/tyler-trents-cells-lead-to-groundbreaking-therapy

Peace & Community Can Accomplish Greatness

While this is just his individual contribution, he inspired a community through his calm and peace in the face of enormous challenges. He showed that united communities can do good and have a collective compassion that is a force multiplier.

It is a responsibility to respond in moments like these. I have been blessed to have the audience I have of Purdue sports fans. After the 49–20 upset that Purdue pulled in that football game over #2 Ohio State, I was approached by a company called Breaking T. They wanted to produce a T-shirt to commemorate the game, since it was the biggest upset Purdue had pulled off in decades and have us sell it on our website. I was more than happy to do so, but I had a responsibility. I couldn't fathom profiting off that night for what it meant to Tyler and the Purdue community, so I agreed to donate every cent we made on commission to the Walther Cancer Research Foundation.

I thought we would sell a few shirts and be able to donate a hundred dollars at best. Well, we sold several hundred shirts, and I was able to donate $1,128.36 to the foundation, which was then matched by an endowment to double its impact.

I have been in the building when Purdue basketball has won a Big Ten Championship. I have been to the Rose Bowl. I can honestly say that seeing that donation go out because of the generosity of our readers was the most humbling and amazing thing I have been a part of within our little Purdue community. Our web community has also responded in other ways over the years, most notably in the EDSBS Charity Bowl I mentioned in Chapter 2. I have long viewed this as part of my responsibility to give back because I have been given so much. To be able to do it is an extraordinary honor.

Peace is difficult to achieve in life, but when we find it, it has a centering effect. There is no shame in getting peace where you find it. I find it in the cacophony of a raging Mackey Arena even though the opposing team certainly does not. I have also found it in the quiet of nature while kayaking in the rain in Alaska, while sitting on the beach with a cold drink in hand, and in the mountains of Colorado just to name a few places. Peace is centering. It is a place where we can gather ourselves and think for a moment, or even not think because some quiet in the maelstrom of my mind is a rare treat. It is a place where our minds can rest and recharge. It is also a place where we can let go of our emotions and seek the wisdom we need to proceed.

Wherever you find your peace, seize on it. It is another jumping off point on the path to compassionate living. When we have peace, it is a place

Compassion

to give thanks to God for that peace and our other blessings. Even at the last Supper, before everything fell apart for the Disciples, Jesus spoke of peace:

> 32 Behold, the hour is coming, indeed it has come, when you will be scattered, each to his own home, and will leave me alone. Yet I am not alone, for the Father is with me. 33 I have said these things to you, that in me you may have peace. In the world you will have tribulation. But take heart; I have overcome the world."—John 16:32–33

What immediately followed was not a time of peace. As promised, the disciples were scattered. Peter would deny Jesus. He would be crucified and resurrected, but even then, there wasn't peace. Once they were commissioned to spread the Gospel all the disciples except John were eventually martyred for their faith. Their world was the very definition of tribulation.

But they endured. They were promised peace, and even though this was 2,000 years ago and I never met them, I'd imagine they had that promised peace. They took the teachings of a carpenter from the backwater of the backwater part of the Roman Empire and spread them as far as they could carry them. Those teachings eventually reached Rome and would change the world. Even in their own personal sacrifices, where many of them never saw the Gospel spread as far as it would spread, they had peace because that is what kept them going in their task. They were planting seeds for a harvest they would never see.

This just shows that we can do better when we are united in a common goal. When I cover sporting events, I can see fans united in a common goal of cheering on their teams regardless of their backgrounds, but that only seems to last as long as the event is going on. For many, they are in community with their church, but that community goes away once the Sunday morning service is over. The message they may hear is good, but when they need to go out into the world, they fail to practice the things that the message tells them to do.

Unfortunately, I don't know how to unite people in peace. We have just lived through more than two years of an event that should have united people in a common goal, but instead it only fostered further division, less peace, and little compassion towards our fellow man. Pandemics don't care about political affiliation, race, or background. This COVID-19 pandemic was dispassionate and struck evenly regardless of beliefs. It should have united us in one common goal, but instead less than a month in the selfish

Peace & Community Can Accomplish Greatness

nature of people was already showing that doing something for the common good that might slightly inconvenience others was madness.

And it only got worse from there.

The goal is still to do better individually. It must begin with the moments of peace you find, be it in a deafening basketball arena or in the quiet patter of rain in a kayak near Ketchikan, Alaska. Find that peace, use it to reset yourself, take a moment to be thankful in prayer, ask for wisdom to discover what you can do, and take it back to the communities that you're a part of.

Maybe then we can have some real change.

17

. . . And Justice for All

JUSTICE IS A DIFFICULT topic to think about. All I see is a complete lack of it. If you have enough money and power, you can avoid most serious consequences. Just a few short months ago we had a President literally encourage an insurrection against the government as a last-ditch attempt to keep himself in power and within days those that had the power to mete out actual consequences for his actions were already handwashing and letting him get away with it scot free, setting the stage for the next attempt that will come because there were no consequences. Situations like that leave me deeply frustrated, both because there is no real justice in the moment, and it only sets the stage for further injustice down the road.

The amount of injustice in the world is overwhelming. It is not even a matter of punishment. It is a matter of people not even facing the most basic of consequences for their actions because of the power they wield. It is getting worse, and that is not even in a "this is a sign of the End Times" that is almost relished by those enthusiasts. Even if we are living in the End Times, the official End is not currently here, so I feel we cannot stand by and watch the world burn. Fighting injustice is a form of compassion, and, as always, it is something we are called to do.

The summer of 2020 was a tumultuous one. The murder of George Floyd by police in Minneapolis sparked nationwide protests not seen since 1968. Despite a worldwide pandemic going on, people rose up and cried out against injustice because they were frustrated and had enough. It wasn't just George Floyd. It was countless others like Breonna Taylor, Ahmaud Arbery, Philando Castille, and more. There are not enough pages to list the names of every person that suffered similar injustices of being murdered by police, and the fact that Floyd's killer is one of very few that faced actual consequences is cold comfort.

Anna Bright, a minister and educator in Walterboro, SC, wrote about what the Bible says regarding social injustice:

> "When any group in society is oppressed or suffering and is constantly denied the privileges and rights of the institutions that the majority enjoys, it is social injustice. Therefore, it is unfair and will ultimately lead to contention, discord and uprisings, such as what we are seeing now across the globe. A lack of basic human rights, systemic racism, police brutality, a broken criminal justice system, a disparity in funding of public schools, unequal access to healthcare and religious oppression are among the many social injustices that are in dire need of attention in order to ensure freedom, justice, and equality for all citizens in America."
>
> "Sin is sin, no matter who commits it; therefore, social injustice is wrong and should not be tolerated because the Word says, "But glory, honour and peace, to every man that worketh good, to the Jew first, and also to the Gentile: For there is no respect of persons with God." (Romans 2:10–11)"[1]

She goes on to list several other verses supporting the concept of social justice, even as basic as "Do unto others as they would do unto you" from Matthew 7. It seems like a simple concept, yet even with video of a police officer kneeling on George Floyd's neck you still had very vocal support for the officer and people felt that it was *he* that suffered an injustice.

Where is the compassion in that? Refusing to see social injustice in this country is willful ignorance from those that have never felt a single moment of actual oppression in their lives. I apologize for being that blunt, but it is true. It is a refusal to see not only the present-day state of affairs, but the history of this country and how we got to this point. It goes from the Trans-Atlantic slave trade, to slavery being enshrined in the Constitution, to an actual war fought to end it, to the state-sanctioned segregation of society that lasted in the South for most of a century once said war was over, to the present day when people have to take to the streets and demand

---

1. Bright, Anna—The Bible speaks of getting involves to correct social justice—Walterboro Live—https://walterborolive.com/stories/the-bible-speaks-of-getting-involved-to-correct-social-injustice,32424

Compassion

justice because they are tired of people being murdered by police without any consequences.

The defiance, even the violence, of protestors is a cry for compassion. I understand and empathize with them. They have tried other channels to enact real, lasting change and have been denied, so of course they are angry and want to break things. It is one of the few avenues left they have to get people to pay attention. I think of Black Lives Matter activist Kimberly Latrice Jones in this regard:

> "You broke the contract when you killed us in the streets and didn't give a f***. You broke the contract when for 400 years, we played your game and built your wealth. You broke the contract when we built our wealth again on our own by our bootstraps in Tulsa and you dropped bombs on us, when we built it in Rosewood and you came in and you slaughtered us. You broke the contract. So f*** your Target. F*** your Hall of Fame. Far as I'm concerned, they could burn this b**** to the ground, and it still wouldn't be enough. And they are lucky that what black people are looking for is equality and not revenge."[2]

This is such a powerful, impassioned speech she made in support of the Black Lives Matter protests. I am a white male that has never had to suffer any form of real oppression and I am angry for her. I can't even begin to imagine what it is like to actually face what African Americans have faced, and continue to face, over the last several centuries here.

The closest I can think of it is my wife and mother-in-law's experience as a Hispanic woman. After the 2016 election my mother-in-law, who has been in this country for more than 40 years, received a threatening letter on her door that basically said, "Now that Trump is in charge, you are all getting sent back to your own countries." This was in the highest Spanish-speaking city per capita in the nation! I am proud to say that since then she has gotten her citizenship and voted for the first time in 2020, at age 75, and her experience is still nothing compared to what others have experienced.

When we look at what Jesus said about injustice, we see a picture of compassion that I have very little doubt would be on the side of BLM today. His most famous example was in Matthew 25:

---

2. Latrice Jones, Kimberly—Kimberly Latric Jones BLM Video Speech Transcript—https://www.rev.com/blog/transcripts/kimberly-latrice-jones-blm-video-speech-transcript

41 "Then he will say to those on his left, 'Depart from me, you cursed, into the eternal fire prepared for the devil and his angels. **42** For I was hungry and you gave me no food, I was thirsty and you gave me no drink, **43** I was a stranger and you did not welcome me, naked and you did not clothe me, sick and in prison and you did not visit me.' **44** Then they also will answer, saying, 'Lord, when did we see you hungry or thirsty or a stranger or naked or sick or in prison, and did not minister to you?' **45** Then he will answer them, saying, 'Truly, I say to you, as you did not do it to one of the least of these, you did not do it to me.' **46** And these will go away into eternal punishment, but the righteous into eternal life."—Matthew 25:41–46

This is the judgement reserved for the end of time, but I think is serves more as a warning and a call for compassion as opposed to a threat. It shows that we are given ample opportunity to show compassion in this world and it is our choice to not practice it. It is established that we are given free will, but part of that free will doesn't mean our choices are always the best.

We are called to fight injustice because we are called to be compassionate. This goes back to the book of Jeremiah in the Old Testament:

> "Thus says the Lord: Do justice and righteousness, and deliver from the hand of the oppressor him who has been robbed. And do no wrong or violence to the resident alien, the fatherless, and the widow, nor shed innocent blood in this place. For if you will indeed obey this word, then there shall enter the gates of this house kings who sit on the throne of David, riding in chariots and on horses, they and their servants and their people. But if you will not obey these words, I swear by myself, declares the Lord, that this house shall become a desolation."—Jeremiah 22:3–5

Both the Old and New Testament make it clear that we are to fight injustice. Unfortunately, injustice often exists because people refuse to see it. It exists because to recognize it might mean admitting you are wrong. It exists because it might mean you have to make a sacrifice for the greater good to bring about real change. It exists because it might mean you have to give up your wealth, your power, your control, or do something that makes you feel uncomfortable. It exists because acknowledging it might mean taking a deeper look at oneself.

For real change to happen, these things must be done. We must take a deeper, more compassionate look and make changes within ourselves. It's going to be uncomfortable, but real growth often is uncomfortable.

Compassion

Righting a wrong means first admitting that there is a wrong, and that is not easily done.

There are two more instances that stand out to me regarding His idea of justice: They are the story about clearing the Temple and the story about His mercy for the thief on the Cross next to him.

Let's look at the clearing of the temple. It appears in three of the four Gospels: Matthew, Luke, and John. All three accounts are very similar to each other. They have Jesus referring to those changing money in the Temple as a "den of robbers". The victims of his anger were men who were selling doves, sheep, oxen, and other sacraments directly in the Temple. To know why this was happening, you have to look back at Jewish Law. It was based on the Torah, which are, in a sense, the first five books of the Christian Bible.

This includes a lengthy list of various laws, many of which deal with atonement for various sins committed. These sins required a sacrifice, often of birds, sheep, oxen, other livestock, etc. These sacrifices needed to be made in the Temple by the priest on behalf of the people seeking atonement. Now what is easier: buying a sheep, dove, or other animal once you get there, or carrying them around? Also, what would be more valuable to a first century farmer: livestock or money?

By having the livestock directly in the Temple, it was a blasphemy on both sides. For the person seeking atonement, they were sacrificing money instead of something that was likely more valuable, thus it was less of a sacrifice. For the priests, they were making money off something that was supposed to be a sacred practice. No wonder Jesus was angry and seeking justice! He spoke regularly about salvation and grace being given freely, out of compassion. As Matthew 5:17 says, "Do not think that I have come to abolish the Law or the Prophets; I have not come to abolish them but to fulfill them."

That same theme carries over to the thief on the cross. Here was a man that was, in the eyes of everyone, a sinner. He was facing the consequences for his actions. Death was imminent for him, and there would be no chance for him to seek atonement. We don't even know if he was Jewish and attempted to follow the same laws and traditions. He is known as a thief, and that's it.

The opposite thief called for Jesus to use his powers as Messiah and save all three of him. The penitent thief, however, was open. He confessed of his crimes. He knew death was coming, and he asked only to be remembered by Jesus. He is then told by Jesus that, "today you will be with me in paradise."

The difference here is striking. The priests in the Temple had the power to forgive sins as outlined by Jewish law, so they sought to profit off it. Jesus, however, wanted no profit. He was there forgive freely and compassionately. That was a threat to those with power, because if that happened, they would lose it. It does not take much to see this happening in the present day, but we see how Jesus exercised the ability to mete out justice given to Him in both cases. He made it clear that Salvation was to be given freely, with no strings attached.

We are called to seek justice while also being compassionate. Romans 12:19 says "Beloved, never avenge yourselves, but leave it to the wrath of God, for it is written, 'Vengeance is mine, I will repay, says the Lord.'" We see God handing out justice in Scripture by raining down sulfur on Sodom or in the plagues of Egypt. We don't wait for Him to show up and handle things though. He'll do that on a cosmic scale, and we see it in the promised judgement after we die (where remember, Jesus is our mediator).

That doesn't mean we let justice die here on earth. We are called to seek justice and be just in our character. Proverbs 21:3 says, "To do righteousness and justice is more acceptable to the Lord than sacrifice." We are to seek justice in matters where it is clear there is wrongdoing. If we see someone murder someone else then clearly, we have to do something. There is currently injustice in this country and there always has been. Part of what we see today is people finally doing something about it. With our character, however, only God knows our true hearts. I cannot condemn anyone to hell because of something I don't like about them, but neither can anyone else, as much as they would like to.

Finally, justice is a form of compassion. It can be a harsh lesson, but in the long run, a necessary and good one. It is better to teach a child there are consequences for actions early on, but being fair and just in said consequences, than to allow them to go unfettered through life thinking the rules do not apply to them. It is better to have appropriate consequences now as opposed to later in life, when the consequences from injustice are much more severe.

We serve a God that has a compassionate heart. We are given many chances in life to do the right thing, and in the long run, justice will be served by Him. He forgives freely to all. We don't get to decide His long-term justice like we're bouncers at the gates of heaven, but we are to make sure that justice thrives in this life.

18

Speaking of All These Yesterdays

THROUGHOUT THIS BOOK I have implored you to "Do something", mostly because Jesus Himself asked us to do the same. He was not the only one to do it either, though He was obviously the most important. Adam was called to care for the Garden of Eden and start humanity. Noah was supposed to build a boat. Abraham was challenged to have faith. Moses was charged with leading the Israelites to freedom. The list continues on and on through John the Revelator being told to write down a real trippy story about the end of the world and spread it far and wide, resulting in more Kirk Cameron films.

With the Bible, we are given a truth and told to speak on it. What that definition is varies depends on who you speak to. There are so many ways to look at the Bible, and I feel like Jason and Emily Kirk of the Vacation Bible School Podcast describe it very well with how they do their show:

> "We're former Sunday school kids who are going back through the whole Bible, treating it as literature, history, mythology, comedy, pop culture, and everything else. And religion too, I guess! Over and over, we find the Bible is so much better, weirder, deeper, funnier, smarter, and more entertaining than we were ever led to believe."[1]

---

1. Kirk, Jason & Emily—The VBS Podcast—https://www.patreon.com/VBSpodcast/membership

Speaking of All These Yesterdays

The Bible is such a fascinating work because it is contradictory, was written over hundreds of years and tells a story that lasts over thousands of years. Even with a central message it has had people fighting over it forever. It has dozens of contexts and the vision it presents of God is one colored by the time each part was written in, the part of the world it came from, and the experience of those writing down the words. Even the various translations over the centuries have added color to it.

Darrell Bock of the Dallas Theological Seminary has an excellent one-sentence summary of the Bible: "The Bible tells how the loving Creator God restored a lost humanity and cosmos through reestablishing His rule through Jesus Christ and the provision of life to His honor."[2] There are contradictions and confusing messages throughout. The Old Testament has an angry God, one so angry that the Twitter handle "Crazy Old Testament God" was popular before it was suspended. Still, the larger message of reconciliation through Christ comes through.

The Old Testament is a collection of stories that show how man can never measure up to God's impossible standards. We cannot be perfect, and we cannot reconcile ourselves to Him. Writer Adam Hamilton brilliantly sums this up on his blog:

> "The point of the first half of this book was to recognize the complexity of the Bible and to help you see its humanity. If we understand the Bible as having been essentially dictated by God, then yes, we have no choice but to accept what is written as accurately describing God's actions and God's will. But if we recognize the Bible's humanity—that it was written by human beings whose understanding and experience of God was shaped by their culture, their theological assumptions, and the time in which they lived—then we might be able to say, "In this case, the biblical authors were representing what they believed about God rather than what God actually inspired them to say." If we use Jesus's words, and his great commandments, as a colander, we'll see that these violent passages in the Hebrew Bible contradict not only these great commands, but the very life and ministry of Jesus who was God's unmitigated Word."[3]

---

2. Ortlund, Dane—What's the Message of the Bible in One Sentence—*Strawberry-Rhubarb Theology*—http://dogmadoxa.blogspot.com/2011/01/whats-message-of-bible-in-one-sentence.html

3. Hamilton, Adam—God's Violence in the Old Testament Part 2: Possible Solutions—https://www.adamhamilton.com/blog/gods-violence-in-the-old-testament-part-2-possible-solutions#.YVygXxDMLop

Compassion

The New Testament is different. It offers the plan for salvation through Jesus and presents a vastly different view of God. Even if you believe that Jesus was real, but not the Son of God, you must admit that His message was revolutionary not just for His day, but by the way it spread to all corners of the globe. I tried to explain this in Chapter 10, but the very idea of "a Savior for all mankind" when half the world wasn't even known at that point was pretty wild. That it became the dominant religion around the world (and one of three branches from the Abrahamic tradition that represents even more of the globe) is remarkable even if it happened by blind luck instead of a divine plan.

We owe this to the Great Commission:

> "**16** Then the eleven disciples went to Galilee, to the mountain where Jesus had told them to go. **17** When they saw him, they worshiped him; but some doubted. **18** Then Jesus came to them and said, "All authority in heaven and on earth has been given to me. **19** Therefore go and make disciples of all nations, baptizing them in the name of the Father and of the Son and of the Holy Spirit, **20** and teaching them to obey everything I have commanded you. And surely I am with you always, to the very end of the age."— Matthew 28:16–20

This was one of the final things that Jesus told His disciples. They were told to go and tell the world. Human beings enjoy a great story. We learn from them. We grow from them. Stories can be entertaining. They can be cautionary tales. They can teach us. Yes, the disciples told the basics of Jesus' story in that His sacrifice was for all mankind, but if that was all they said we would know so much less than we do now. We wouldn't know of Jesus' humanity. We wouldn't know of the parables He told that still teach us lessons today. We wouldn't know about the values that he tried to spread that affect us here in the real world before we get to enjoy the benefits of eternal life as the result of His sacrifice.

Much of modern Christianity seems to have lost sight of this. There is a lot of, "believe and you'll be saved, but *only* if you believe as I do." We see conditions that are put on salvation, and I don't see conditions as something that we can set on it. Jesus called for us to care for the destitute, heal the sick, turn away from greed, love the sinner, and a bunch of other things I don't see from people who are Christians today. They may be in the technical, "I believe in the way, the truth, and the light," sense, but in terms of practicing many of the lessons of Jesus they are far off.

Speaking of All These Yesterdays

In her work *Native* author Kaitlin B. Curtice speaks about how modern American Christianity has turned away from this:

> I call myself a Christian, and yet, how do I reckon with settler colonial Christianity that is influenced by empire? We are taught about who Jesus is, but in Western Christianity we are taught a diluted, whitewashed version. Settler colonial Christianity puts itself at the center of everything as the sole power, and evangelism becomes a tool used to erase other cultures and religions from the people whom Christians are meant to serve. Settler colonial Christianity is a religion that takes, that demeans the earth and the oppressed, and that holds people in these systems without regard for how Jesus treated people.[4]

Jesus preached a message of compassion. I know I have said that many times in a variety of ways, but that is what it boils down to. He preached compassion, so we're supposed to practice it. We're also supposed to speak of it through not only our words, but through our actions. We're not going to be perfect when we do it, either. Lord knows I have not been perfect in writing this, but I felt called to write a few things down and it is up to God to convey my message in the right way. All we can do is speak our truth and hope that it makes a difference.

We are defined by our stories. We use them to connect with people and show that we are caring, empathetic individuals. I've always felt that had a unique type of courtship (if you would call it that) with my wife. In 2002 the idea of dating via the internet was quite revolutionary, and even scary. I don't know if there were dating sites yet, but the idea of meeting a complete stranger off the internet was considered to be a little crazy, maybe even dangerous. America Online had been around for several years, however, and the proliferation of AOL Instant Messenger made it easier and easier to communicate with people. At that point it was only a matter of time before online dating became more commonplace.

I had a very good friend from a few writing classes that turned me on to a site called Open Diary. This was one of the very early blogging sites, but it wasn't marketed as a blog. It was a place to write down thoughts like a regular diary, only it was shared openly. I can't even remember when I started it, but I wrote in it regularly, mostly about finishing college, going out into the real world, and about silly basketball stuff.

---

4. Curtice, Kaitlin B.—*Native*—Brazos Press, 2020

Compassion

The platform was nice because you could leave comments on other people's diaries, but only if you were a writer of one yourself. You could also follow other people you found interesting. In May of 2002 I received a comment from a woman who lived in Miami and had also just recently graduated from college. We had a shared experience of not knowing what to do next with our lives and having trouble finding a job in a poor job market. We were also big sports fans, so there was a connection there.

We connected through our stories. Even if we simply wrote about how our day went there was a connection there. When you're unemployed you have a lot of free time and you keep weird hours, especially in your early 20s, so our stories were often posted at odd times. I do remember waiting with quite a bit of anticipation to read her latest post so I could comment, even if it meant reading it at 2:30am while I watched the World Cup being played in South Korea and Japan because I wasn't working the next day.

Eventually those stories led to the next step: actually making a phone call. I remember it was a big day when she announced she had gotten a cell phone (yes, there was a time when you could be in your early 20s and NOT have a cell phone) and I could call her. That only led to more stories. We were able to speak with each other almost nightly for months until she finally had the crazy idea to come see me.

It took an incredible amount of faith for her to get on a plane, fly to Indiana, and meet some random guy off the internet (at a hotel, no less, because I had finally gotten a job and couldn't get there in time to meet her at the airport), but it would not have happened if not for our stories. We shared a common past. We connected through our experience. We also practiced compassion for the circumstances we were going through at the time. If you fast forward 15 years a meeting like that is much more common, but at the time it was an incredible leap of faith.

Within a year she had decided to uproot her life and move to Indiana. Within three years we were married, and now we have been for over 17 years and our son is the greatest gift God could give us. It has not been easy. I know it is a tired trope to say marriage isn't easy, but there have been some incredibly rough moments we have had to work through (and are still working through!). Still, all of it doesn't happen without being open to speak about our truths, our stories, and our experiences. I am sure one day our son will appreciate it too since it led to his very existence.

I don't think this is very different from the way Jesus first propagated His message. He was very big on parables. The gospel of Luke alone contains

Speaking of All These Yesterdays

24 parables, 18 of which do not appear in any other gospel. Matthew has 23, 11 of which are unique. Mark only has eight, two of which are unique, while it is disputed as to what counts as a parable in the gospel of John, as many of those stories are allegories.

Regardless, storytelling and relating to people on an individual level was critical to Christ's public ministry. Not only that, but it is also how He was able to instruct the disciples for the important work ahead of them. It was His way of connecting with people. The larger focus was to get people to focus on God and His kingdom. When you investigate them there is a certain shared experience, and it is in that connection that we learn.

We know a mustard seed is small and the tree it produces is large, so it is not a long step from there to a parable about faith. People in the First Century knew about how to mend clothes since they were limited in their wardrobes, so the parable of the old garment was a way to relate to people. Yes, Christ could have lectured his disciples like a professor, simply dropping knowledge on them and expecting them to keep up, but these parables were a way to connect with their real lives and make the message he was speaking more personal.

This is why speaking on our yesterdays is so important. We are called to spread the gospel but standing on a street corner and shouting "You're going to hell if you don't repent" is not very effective. There is a guy that does this when we go to Cincinnati for Reds games, and most of his literature ends up scattered on the sidewalk close to the stadium. He is at best ignored by thousands of fans that walk past him. The best way is to relate to people. Get to know their story. Be compassionate. Speak on your own yesterdays and truly connect with them.

19

Thank You for Listening

ONE OF MY FAVORITE bands is HURT. The lead singer is a man named J. Loren Wince, and he is a classically trained musician that is incredibly talented. I have seen several of their shows and J. not only sings, but he plays lead guitar and, on some songs, shows off his musical prowess by playing the violin. Each song is not written. They are crafted, as you can tell he pours himself into every note.

The final song on the band's second album is titled, "Thank You for Listening," and even though it is not the band's last song as they made a few more albums after it, the song caps a two album duology that is titled "Volume I" and "Volume II", respectively. It is the capper of 23 songs that feel completely interconnected, and it serves as an epic coda that encapsulates what writing this book has felt like. I wasn't sure where it was going when I started writing down basic notes and thoughts while sitting on the balcony of a beach house overlooking the Gulf of Mexico from Dauphin Island, Alabama. I didn't even know if it would become a book. I felt a calling and I knew I needed to act on it. You cannot stick the perfect landing if you don't first jump, so I decided to jump. I don't know if I stuck the landing or tumbled ass over teakettle, but this has been a learning experience. It has also been just what I needed, like J. says in the song.

It all goes back to the principle of "Do Something". It was both the impetus for writing this as well as a way of spreading compassion in a world that has lost it. I couldn't sit idly by and complain about the world. I had to do something. Since my strength is my ability to write that is where the calling led me.

We are not going to get back to living with compassion in society without doing something about it. That takes individual effort because we can only control ourselves. That is the first step. We must be willing to open our own eyes and step outside of our own zones of comfort to meet others where they are, not make them come to where we are. We must be willing to see different views and different experiences. We must be open to other people's pain in order to be compassionate.

My cynical nature leads me to think often that there is no hope in this world. Donald Trump is out of office, but it is clear he is running again and could win, making things significantly worse when he is bent on revenge with no one willing to stop him because they are too cowardly. Climate change is real, and we can still do something about it, but it would cost money and mean sacrifices for people, so we must argue about it as it creeps. We see news of school shootings, but collectively do nothing to prevent them.

I tried to write this book because I felt we could somehow get back to connecting and communicating compassionately instead of endless bickering and attacks. I did this because I have seen my own personal relationships suffer as the result of this factioning and radicalization. I wanted to say, "ENOUGH!" and hopefully show that there can be a difference way. Maybe it was in vain, but I must hope it wasn't.

In the introduction I spoke about *Jesus & John Wayne* by Kristen Kobes du Mez and how it does such an excellent job of how we got here. She recently did an interview with Anne Helen Peterson about her book, and I found her take on hope fascinating:

> "To be honest, I still don't have a lot of hope right now. The hope that I do have comes in large part from the remarkable response to the book in conservative evangelical spaces. I've heard from hundreds and hundreds of readers who share with me, often in exquisite detail, how their own stories map onto the narrative I tell in Jesus and John Wayne. I've heard from sexual and spiritual abuse survivors who feel validated to see their stories placed at the center of our narratives, not covered up or sidelined. I've heard from people who tried and failed to live up to the ideals of purity culture, and from people who shaped their marriages around patriarchal authority and female submission, often with devastating consequences. I've also heard from a number of evangelicals

who have held varying degrees of leadership who are now deeply convicted in their own complicity in propping up these abusive systems. These are the conversations that give me hope. The individual reckoning is real, and I've seen many conservative evangelicals risk jobs, friendships, and family relationships to call for change."[1]

I like the way she pictures hope. It is not by a massive rebuke by Evangelicals en masse, but of those peeling away as they see what is happening and finally get it. I pray for this daily. I pray that those in my life corrupted by this false message finally see it and return to the principles they value. I cannot bring down Focus on the Family, Franklin Graham, Liberty University, or any of the other larger forces that have given rise to this warped version of Christianity. That is too strong and powerful for just one person, and those powers have been entrenched for decades.

There is still that "Do Something" mentality though, and it begins with living compassionately while working within my own circles:

- **Know What You Believe In And Why**—Don't just take what others say and put it on for yourself while following blindly. Do your own research (and please, for the love of God, do it outside of Facebook and all social media). Ask questions. Always be ready to seek knowledge.

- **Make Small Acts**—Grand gestures are good, but they can be difficult to pull off and it takes a lot of outside factors to make them have a huge impact. Small acts are more intentional. They show you care and can be personalized for the audience. Even if it is simply a note in your spouse's lunch it shows you are intentional, and even begins to change your own thinking.

- **Be Humble**—Jesus was the ultimate example of humility. He was the freaking Son of God for crying out loud! He could have rolled into Jerusalem with Stormbreaker like Thor in *Avengers: Infinity War*. Instead, he took on the form of a bondservant to the point of death. Swallow your pride and submit yourself in the service of others.

- **Have Grace**—My dad is fond of saying that the only perfect person ever was nailed to a Cross. We all screw up. We all have to deal with people

---

1. Petersen, Anne Helen—Jesus and John Wayne and Mel's Gibson's William Wallace from the Movie Braveheart—*Culture Study*—https://annehelen.substack.com/p/jesus-and-john-wayne

who screw up. Having the grace to look past that and still reach out to others is not a weakness. Also, remember to have grace with yourself.

- **Be Grateful**—Always take a moment to pause and reflect on what blessings you have been given, even if it is hard to do so. No matter where you are in life, there is always something to be thankful for. Seek that thankfulness and use it to center yourself in the face of your trials.

- **Remember That God Is Huge**—He is bigger than we can possibly imagine. He controls the entire universe, and His plans are not going to be undone by anything we do here. They also are not going to be accelerated by anything we do. We don't fully understand God and never will, but He is in control. He can handle anything, even if it is your anger at Him.

- **Life has Consequences**—Even if we seek truth it can come with a cost. Consequences can be a sign of compassion because they present a chance for us to learn and grow. We have to be willing to do so.

- **"I Don't Know" Is Okay**—We don't know everything. We *won't* know everything. The sooner we admit that the better we live, and it is okay to tell people that too. It gives us a chance to learn together.

- **Be Willing To Serve**—This connects with humility, but always be ready to serve and help. Be willing to be there for people and hear their pain. Do what it takes to aid them, even at the cost of yourself. Shut up and listen when someone else needs to talk.

- **Persevere**—As former North Carolina State basketball coach Jim Valvano said in his ESPY's speech while dying of cancer, "Don't give up. Don't EVER give up."[2] Endure. Persevere. Seek people who will help you do so.

- **Learn From Tests**—I am not talking about a math test or the SAT. I am talking about those times in life where circumstances are trying to teach you a lesson. Ask questions of yourself in those moments and be open to those lessons.

- **Love Freely And Deeply**—We cannot have compassion without love. It is impossible. There are many different types of love, but compassion and caring are at the center of all of them. Let it fuel your ability to love.

2. Jimmy V's ESPYs Speech Annotated—https://www.espn.com/espn/feature/story/_/id/24087641/jimmy-v-espys-speech-annotated

Compassion

- **Forgive When You Can't Forget**—This is slightly different from grace. Grace is a form of patience that if given freely. Forgiveness takes a personal sacrifice because you know you will not forget why you need to forgive. It is a specific action and form of compassion.

- **Seek Wisdom And Apply It**—Wisdom is different from knowledge because it is the proper application of knowledge through experience. It is not infallible, but it will end up taking you a long way. Also, don't be afraid to pause and reflect. Prayer is a powerful tool and the time spent in reflection is critical. There is no set format for prayer, either, and expressing your anger to God can be cathartic. He can take it.

- **Live In Community**—We all have different social circles and communities. They are inescapable but caring for the people in them is critical. Remember to be selfless and serve so you can help everyone in these connections grow.

- **Seek Justice**—We must pursue what is right. There is far too much injustice in the world and to not fight it is pretty much saying that you're okay with it. Stand up in the face of what is wrong for those who cannot stand up. Add your power to those that do stand up.

- **Tell Your Stories**—We connect through our stories. Be willing to share yours and be willing to listen to others so you can forge these connections. Never be afraid to share your truth. Always be prepared to listen.

I have a lot of regrets in my life. I am not perfect, and I fully expect that you, dear reader, have not agreed with me on everything I have put down here. That's okay. Even admitting that is okay is part of my appeal to get back to compassionate living. I have tried to be raw and share my experiences in the hope that my mistakes can be a lesson to others or even encourage them if they have made similar mistakes. All I wanted to do was to try and make a difference in the world and get people to think. I want them to see that we can do better. We can expect better. We can BE better.

And I thank you for listening.

About the Author

TRAVIS MILLER IS THE founder and site manager of Hammer & Rails: an SB Nation community dedicated to covering the Purdue Boilermakers. He is a 2002 graduate of Purdue and can often be found in West Lafayette or wherever Purdue football and basketball are playing. He has seen the Cubs win a World Series in his lifetime so he knows that nothing is impossible in the world. He currently lives in Indianapolis with his wife, son, and cat.

Acknowledgements

FIRST OFF, I CANNOT believe that I am here working on an acknowledgements page. I didn't even know if this would ever get outside of a few pages of a notebook, let alone into a real book that people might buy, so first off, thank you, reader. If you've made it this far you have put up with a strange person in myself. I hope you're better for it, somehow.

I want to thank both of my parents. My dad is a man of deep faith and I admire him for it. He has instilled many of the values in me that allow me to take the stands I do. We may not agree on a lot these days, but he has been a great, loving father and I am forever appreciative of him. For my mom, you are an inspiration for being your own woman. You raised my older sister as a single mom for a time, sacrificed much for your kids, and supported me unquestionably in everything. I continue to admire your strength and will.

I want to thank my high school friends: Matt and Donna Stalter, Roman Underwood, Tyson Neal, Terry Husband, and Cayte Hiers. You have all pushed me when I needed to be pushed and were patient with me when I was being "me".

Thank you to Greg Compton, a former co-worker who has been an excellent friend, mentor to this whole dad experience since he is a wonderful father to his two boys, and a great sounding board when I just need someone to talk to. May your Sunday morning guitar solos at your church

Acknowledgements

always rock. Thank you also for turning me to the Southeast Project and Ryan's teachings.

Thank you to my staff at HammerandRails.com, my Purdue website: Andrew Ledman, Andrew Holmes, Drew Schneider, Kyle Holderfield, Casey Bartley, Jace Jellison, Rachel Van Gessel, and Dr. Juan Crespo (a retired writer). Without you I wouldn't have anywhere near the audience I have to write about Purdue sports, which is what led to this. Thank you for your support in this side endeavor.

A very big thank you to the folks in the Vacation Bible School Podcast Discord chat. You have all shown me that I am not alone in a lot of my thoughts and feelings. In just a few short months you have helped renew and transform my faith. Thank you also the Commentariat at Underdog Dynasty (formerly the EDSBS Commentariat) for being a great sounding board on life in general.

Thank you very much to Dave Kitchell and David Kasey for giving me a chance as a young 19-year-old green sportswriter. You guys started this. I would not be anywhere close to where I am today without both of you. Also thank you to Bryan Gaskins, the current sports editor at the Kokomo Tribune, and Will Willems, the sports editor at the Lebanon Reporter, for letting me continue my hobby of writing about Indiana high school basketball. Rest in peace, David.

Thank you to my grandparents for the love you had for me and the support for me, especially Raymond Dillon. I have mourned your loss for over 30 years, but still feel you with me. You're the first person I want to meet again in heaven after Jesus. And yes, Someday finally happened with the Cubs.

Thank you to Carol Mooney, Peggy Foust, and JoAnn Miller. My basketball moms and basketball grandmother. Thank you for being great role models as women and for helping instill my love of basketball.

Thank you to fellow writer Paul Banks, who wrote two books of his own and inspired me to write one of my own. Just remember: There are no laws when you're drinking White Claws at Wrigley.

Thank you to Ms. Pamela Steele, my son's day care provider. Thank you for being a woman of such deep faith and for doing the work that you do in taking care of those kids. You are family.

It is silly, but I have to thank my sweet cat, Ventress. She was a pleasant surprise in choosing us in the middle of the pandemic as a scrawny stray who had escaped her foster home and came up on our porch. She is has

Acknowledgements

done so much good for our family and was often my editor, sitting on my lap demanding ear scritches as I wrote. Any typos are her fault.

Finally, and most importantly, thank you to my wife, Liz, and son, Dillon. I am not a perfect man, but you have made me a better man. You have believed in me even when you probably shouldn't have. It was your idea to start that silly blog a long time ago, Liz, and I am forever indebted to you. Thank you for putting up with me, as I know I am a hassle.

And Dillon, you are the greatest gift God has ever given me. I have been in awe of you since the moment I looked at you after you were born and your eyes said, "Hey, I know you. You're daddy." That was the greatest gift you could have given me, and you were only five minutes old. Everything else has been icing. It is a privilege to be your dad.

www.ingramcontent.com/pod-product-compliance
Lightning Source LLC
Chambersburg PA
CBHW050825160426
43192CB00010B/1906